Nancy has done it again. *From Clutter to Clarity* contains the *how* of getting clutter out of your life, instead of just the *why* like so many other books. Nancy uses stories of real people to make her points, which makes this an entertaining and fast read. Tired of feeling busy all the time? Read this book.

DAVE RAMSEY
Best-selling author, nationally acclaimed speaker, syndicated radio host

----------◆----------

From Clutter to Clarity shows women how to simplify their lives in a way that will lead to permanent results. Instead of focusing on the ever-popular quick fixes for the problem of a complicated lifestyle, Nancy helps readers address the real problem: a cluttered heart and mind, which leads to cluttered living. Through personal examples and success stories from other women, Nancy gives readers hope that, with God's help, they can achieve the clarity and meaning in life they desire.

EMILIE BARNES
Internationally acclaimed author, speaker, and organizer

----------◆----------

Inspiring. Challenging. Engaging. In *From Clutter to Clarity* you will discover proven biblical answers for the balanced, fulfilled life you've always wanted. Nancy provides wise spiritual and practical answers to the heartfelt questions all women are asking about living intentionally in the twenty-first century. Finally, here is a book full of relevance to where I have been, where I am, and where I hope to go spiritually.

SHARON HOFFMAN
Inspirational speaker, author of *The G.I.F.T.ed Woman* and *Come Home to Comfort*

----------◆----------

Yes, freedom from the clutter of my world—at last! God makes it possible, Nancy makes it practical. With her wise guidance and tender heart, Nancy helps us take control of our lives, inside and out, to build a more meaningful relationship with God and a simpler, more peaceful walk in the busyness around us.

KARON PHILLIPS GOODMAN
Author of *Another Fine Mess, Lord* and *Pursued by the Shepherd*

----------◆----------

Nancy has provided her readers a fresh perspective on the problem of clutter. She touches on all areas that clutter can dominate—including our walk with God. Her insights will help anyone—even those who have tried other clutter-free approaches.

Jonni McCoy
Author of *Miserly Moms* and *Frugal Families*

from
clutter
to clarity

NANCY TWIGG

from
clutter
to clarity

simplifying life from the inside out

Standard®
PUBLISHING
Bringing The Word to Life

Cincinnati, Ohio

Published by Standard Publishing, Cincinnati, Ohio

www.standardpub.com

Printed in the United States of America

Project editors: Robert Irvin, Lynn Lusby Pratt

Cover design: Brand Navigation

Interior design: Dina Sorn at Ahaa! Design

Special thanks to Norwalk Furniture for assisting with the cover design.

ISBN 978-0-7847-2110-0

Library of Congress Cataloging-in-Publication Data

Twigg, Nancy.
  From clutter to clarity : simplifying life from the inside out / Nancy
Twigg.
      v. cm.
  Contents: An issue of the heart -- A new definition of clutter -- The
clarity principle -- From cluttered thoughts and attitudes to inner clarity --
Finding contentment in a discontented world -- Satisfaction guaranteed --
The secret of a worry-free life -- Letting go of the untrustables -- Seeing
ourselves as God sees us -- From cluttered lifestyle to outer clarity -- No is
not a dirty word -- Too busy for God -- Making peace with our possessions --
Escaping the technology trap -- More is never enough -- From cluttered money
matters to financial clarity -- Living the good life -- Stewardship is more
than giving -- Sweet freedom -- The paradox of giving -- What money cannot
do -- Guard your heart.
  ISBN 978-0-7847-2110-0 (perfect bound)
  1. Christian women--Religious life. 2. Simplicity--Religious
aspects--Christianity. I. Title.

BV4527.T95 2007
248.8'43--dc22

                                                      2007000011

13 12 11 10 09 08 07   9 8 7 6 5 4 3 2 1

*Just as iron sharpens iron, friends sharpen
the minds of each other.*
PROVERBS 27:17 (*CEV*)

✦ DEDICATED TO ✦
all the friends who sharpened my mind
as I worked on this book:

My writers group

My critique group

My prayer support team

My personal prayer partners

And my two best friends, Michael and Lydia

I couldn't have done it without you!

CONTENTS

an issue
of the
heart

Make a clean heart in me, O God.

PSALM 51:10 (*NLV*)

Therefore, since we are surrounded by such a great cloud of witnesses, let us throw off everything that hinders and the sin that so easily entangles, and let us run with perseverance the race marked out for us. Let us fix our eyes on Jesus, the author and perfecter of our faith, who for the joy set before him endured the cross, scorning its shame, and sat down at the right hand of the throne of God.

HEBREWS 12:1, 2

ONE

GOOD-BYE, CLUTTER!

I'm through with outdated ideas about things that no longer serve a purpose in my life. I'm ready to see clutter for what it really is.

---

a new definition of clutter

When my husband, Michael, and I were first getting to know Sonya and Jerry, they often told us stories of problems with past-due bills, overdrawn checking accounts, lost documents, and forgotten appointments. But I didn't understand why they struggled to keep their lives in order—until we helped them move from their apartment into their first home.

On the day we helped them pack, the apartment looked like a tornado had touched down in the middle of their living room. Papers completely covered the floor—expired coupons, old receipts, unopened mail, check stubs from years ago . . . Trinkets and whatnots littered every nook and cranny. Things that seemed important were indiscriminately mixed with things that looked as if they should be trashed. The whole apartment was a cesspool of disorganization.

As we and other friends managed to pack up the mess, we suddenly heard Jerry bellow from the back room: "SONYAAAAAA!!!" Alarmed, we all ran to see what was wrong. There in the bedroom stood Jerry, holding a cooler he had just discovered buried in their closet under a mound of other stuff. Inside was putrid, unidentifiable food left over from the camping trip we'd all taken together eight months earlier!

"Sonya, why didn't you clean this out after our camping trip?" Jerry barked as he made his way toward the door to take the cooler to the Dumpster.

"I thought *you* did," was the best excuse Sonya could muster—before we all burst into laughter.

With so much disorder and disarray in their home, no wonder Sonya and Jerry struggled with the details of life and seemed to go from one crisis to the next. Thankfully, they have become much more organized since then.

When it comes right down to it, the source of much of life's craziness is clutter. Clutter in our minds, in our homes, and in our finances. Think of all the energy and effort you expend each day just dealing with clutter. Think about the emotional stress and strain it causes you. Just like bacon grease poured down the kitchen drain, clutter gunks up the works and keeps life from working well.

Much More Than Old Magazines

Cleaning out closets and drawers is one way to deal with clutter, but clutter is much more than old magazines, outdated clothes, and kitchen gadgets you never use. From now on, think of clutter as any possession, habit, thought pattern, attitude, or activity that (1) you don't need or use anymore, (2) doesn't fit or work for you like it used to, or (3) doesn't add value and meaning to your life as it once did.

Missy has three children, ages twenty, fifteen, and eight. When I told her that I write and speak about living simply, her eyes lit up.

"Oh, Nancy," she said, "I've learned a lot about keeping life simple." She explained that she used to be a perfectionist. She thought that to be a good mom she had to cook elaborate meals, keep her house spotless, and participate in everything that went on at her children's school.

A new definition of clutter: anything that complicates your life and prevents you from living in peace as you live out your purpose.

But by the time her third child was born, Missy realized that trying to do it all no longer brought joy as it once had. Her concept of what it meant to be a good mother no longer fit. Her incredibly high standards only caused stress and anxiety, and Missy discovered that perfectionism was actually a form of clutter she needed to release.

"I learned that you can't do everything," Missy told me. "Besides, no one cares if you do!"

Missy's story illustrates a new definition of clutter: anything that complicates your life and prevents you from living in peace as you live out your purpose. In the past, you may have thought of clutter only in terms of stuff—those size 6 jeans you hope to wear again someday or those unfinished projects in your garage. But let me share a secret with you: unused, unwanted, and unneeded material possessions are only the tip of the iceberg!

What about the multitude of commitments that cram-pack your schedule? What about the thoughts that jumble your mind and the spending habits that sabotage your finances? All of these things are clutter too, because they cause chaos and confusion.

An Issue of the Heart

Have you ever tried to lug an overstuffed suitcase through a crowded airport? Not an easy task, is it? No matter how hard you try, you simply cannot move quickly and efficiently when you're carrying a heavy load.

Think of clutter as heavy baggage—physical, emotional, and financial baggage that weighs you down, holds you back, and keeps you from maneuvering effectively through your life. Our suitcases are filled with all kinds of deadweight: habits we need to give up, attitudes we've long since outgrown, and activities and possessions that no longer serve a reasonable purpose. If you want to lighten your load and move from clutter to clarity, you have to eliminate some of the junk.

Our suitcases are filled with all kinds of deadweight: habits we need to give up, attitudes we've long since outgrown, and activities and possessions that no longer serve a reasonable purpose.

What keeps you from moving forward at a steady pace in your life? Maybe you struggle with physical clutter around your home. Try as you might, you cannot seem to get organized. Or maybe you want to get a handle on your finances. You are tired of making good money but having nothing to show for it. Or maybe yours is an issue with time. You are tired of living at warp speed. You want to stop running and start living.

When you think of clutter as anything that complicates your life and prevents you from living in peace as you live out your purpose, you begin to see what a tremendous problem clutter truly is. But the root causes of this ugly clutter make the clutter itself look tame!

Think about it. Why do you say yes to everyone who requests your time and services? Are you afraid you won't be liked you if you say no? Do you feel the need to present a supermom image to the world?

Clutter does more than affect us physically and emotionally; it also affects us spiritually because it keeps us from following Jesus fully.

What about those clothes you hold onto even though you know you will never wear them again? Are you afraid that if you get rid of them you will need them again someday? And if you did happen to need them, do you doubt God's ability to provide more?

Do you have a tendency to spend more than you can afford? Ask yourself why you do that. Are you driven by feelings of discontent or a need for instant gratification? Are you afraid that if you pass on a sale now you will never find a good price on that item again?

You see, clutter goes much deeper than just having a messy desk or disorganized pantry. Clutter is an issue of the heart.

DEADLY DECEPTIONS

Clutter is a problem for anyone, but for Christians it spells major trouble. Clutter does more than affect us physically and emotionally; it also affects us spiritually because it keeps us from following Jesus fully. We simply cannot make room for him when so many other things are in the way. The more we stay focused on the junk of this life, the less time and energy we have to focus on the important matters—God and his plans for our lives.

Satan has been deceiving us from the very beginning. It all started in the Garden of Eden when he misrepresented the truth and tricked Adam and Eve into believing they could actually be as wise as God. Because Adam and Eve were not on guard, they fell for this ploy. To this day, Satan continues his deception and exploitation; he is our constant enemy. Unless we are on guard, we too will fall into his trap. Let's look at some examples of how this works.

Do you have difficulty saying no? Satan knows that we women are wired to be caretakers. We care for our families, our friends, people at work, and people at church. Satan also knows that our self-worth can be closely tied to a need to be needed. We feel best about ourselves when we know others depend on us. Master manipulator that he is, Satan plays on these inborn tendencies and lures us into taking them to the extreme. Before you know it, a natural inclination—helping and caring for others— becomes an unhealthy obsession. We try to do it all, but even noble pursuits become clutter when they endanger our sanity and leave us with no time to connect with God.

Our enemy uses the same kind of tricks in the area of spending. We all enjoy buying the occasional new outfit or decorative piece for our homes. But Satan loves to fool us into thinking we need more stuff to make us happy. He stirs up feelings of inadequacy and worry over what other people think of us. Something that seems benign—like splurging on a treat for yourself—becomes an outward symptom of something harmful going on inside. Before we know it, instant pleasure seems more important than long-term financial stability.

From Clutter to Clarity

Whatever the clutter challenges you face, trust me when I say that you can learn to clarify your life by putting clutter in its place. I know because I have done it.

My clarity training began ten years ago when my husband and I both left comfortable jobs to work for ourselves. In just a matter of weeks, we went from two good incomes to one iffy income from a business just getting started. Suddenly we had to become experts at making our dollars stretch. We learned quickly to tell the difference between a need and a want.

Even noble pursuits become clutter when they endanger our sanity and leave us with no time to connect with God.

We also learned a great deal about getting rid of excess baggage. My biggest clutter challenge was not dealing with cluttered living spaces or even cluttered finances. My challenge was opening up my emotional suitcase and going through its contents carefully. When I did, I discovered all kinds of clutter lurking inside.

I found worry and doubt. I uncovered a faulty self-image and an inability to set appropriate boundaries. I even found an unhealthy preoccupation with what others thought of me.

I learned to trade in these old clunkers, one by one, for the more efficient models God offered. It was a painful process, but necessary.

I'm not saying I have it all together. Believe me, I don't. I'm not saying I never face challenges. Believe me, I do! Is my life perfect? No. But I have come to a place of clarity—where life is peaceful and purposeful and much more pleasant. And isn't that what we all want—to live in peace as we live out our purpose?

If that's what you are looking for, keep reading. We're just getting started.

CLUTTER *BUSTERS*

✦ How do you feel about the new definition of *clutter* in this chapter?

✦ On a continuum from clutter to clarity, where are you today? What are some examples of clutter in your life?

✦ If you were to open the suitcase of your heart today, what kinds of deadweight would you find inside? Describe how life will look after you rid yourself of these encumbrances.

✦ What do you think is happening on the inside to create the clutter in your life?

COMING INTO CLARITY

I actually am one of those hyperorganized people whose calendar includes things like "change toothbrush" every three months and "clean makeup brushes" every four months. I own my own home without a mortgage, have no other debt, and account for literally every penny in my budget. And one thing I've done all my life is stocking up—buying six of everything. I just panic when my storehouses are depleted.

Recently, I have been looking into my heart to declutter it. I've tried to figure out the emotional reason why I want to always have everything I might need at my fingertips. What I realized is that I seem to have an emotional need to be prepared. And I had been trying to deal with this need to be prepared by overbuying. Since I realized this, I am learning to really put my faith in God and not in my own personal storehouses.

Connie
Gulf Shores, Alabama

TWO

GOOD-BYE, CLUTTER!
*No more cluttered heart for me—I'm ready to
tackle the problem at its source.*

---

the
clarity
principle

Several years ago I developed an itchy rash on my left arm; then I began to have severe pain in my neck and shoulder. Simple tasks like putting on a sweater or rolling over in bed were torture. I didn't know what was wrong. I didn't even know if the two symptoms were related. All I knew was that I needed medical attention.

My doctor quickly diagnosed the condition as shingles. She prescribed a medicated patch to relieve the rash and the pain, as well as an oral medication. It seemed to me that putting some kind of medicine on the skin would be enough to clear up a skin problem. But the doctor explained that shingles is not a skin disease; instead, it's actually a nerve disease. When the virus attacks the nerves, the disease typically manifests itself through skin eruptions and pain in the affected area. Treating only the symptoms would not make the problem go away. We had to get rid of the virus that was causing the problem in the first place. We had to attack the ailment at its source.

What an appropriate analogy for clutter! Clutter is an internal disease, a heart condition. Cluttered homes and lives are merely outward representations of what's happening on the inside. The problem is not that you have an overcrowded closet or that your schedule is chronically overbooked. Those are just symptoms. The real predicament is that your heart is cluttered. You can try to treat the symptoms by giving away clothes you don't wear or cutting back on commitments, but the ailment will not go away until you treat it at its source. Until you declutter your heart, any changes you make to your environment will be only temporary.

The only way to truly simplify life and achieve clarity is to deal with clutter from the inside out. If we declutter our hearts and minds first, clarity will begin to show on the outside as well.

CLARITY 101

Think of your life as a course called Clarity 101, with Hebrews 12:1, 2 as the required course reading. Among the theological gems in this passage, we also find what I call the Clarity Principle, a three-part strategy for keeping our lives simple and clearly focused so we are free to live out God's plans for our lives:

THROW OFF WHAT HINDERS YOU. Hebrews 12:1 says, "Let us throw off everything that hinders and the sin that so easily entangles." In other words, if something holds you back in any way, get rid of it! Throw it out. Give it the boot!

Notice that the writer tells us to get rid of not only things that hinder but also the sin that entangles. This is important because the two are so closely related. Satan knows our areas of weakness much better than we do, and he will use anything he can to cause us to stumble and fall. Even things that may seem innocent become sinful when distorted and taken to the extreme.

When I was a teenager, I loved listening to rock music, the heavy metal stuff. I listened to hard rock throughout my teens and even into my adult years. One of the worst arguments Michael and I had while we were dating was about music. We were driving in my car one evening when a song with explicit lyrics came on the radio.

"Now you're messing with a son of a . . ." The words repeated over and over.

"How can you listen to that junk?" Michael demanded. "Don't you find that offensive?"

At the time I was blind to the fact that this was an area of weakness for me. Although I didn't like the words in that particular song, I did like the music, and I was angry that Michael would question my musical taste.

"Why are you so controlling and critical?" I wanted to know. "How dare you be so self-righteous!"

Although it took a few years, I eventually realized Michael was right. As I matured in my faith, I learned that listening to music with questionable messages was a hindrance for me. I couldn't have the mind of Christ if I filled my mind with worldly junk. I finally gave up secular music altogether because I felt that was what God was calling me to do. Doing so simplified my spiritual life tremendously because I was no longer sabotaging my spiritual growth with tainted music. Listening to heavy metal music had always stirred up all kinds of rebellious and lustful feelings inside me. Now the praise music I listen to stirs my spirit with feelings of joy that spur me on to live the way I truly want to live.

PERSEVERE THROUGH THE DIFFICULTIES. In addition to getting rid of hindrances, we are encouraged in Hebrews 12:1

to take another step: "Let us run with perseverance the race marked out for us." The Christian life is a race that tests our endurance, not our speed. This competition is not a 50-yard dash on a smooth track. It's a 26.2-mile marathon with hurdles on hilly terrain. The tricks and traps Satan uses to waylay us can easily take their toll. When difficulties come and we want to quit the race, we must instead become more committed. No one crosses the finish line without making a decision to persevere.

Through the toughest times in our spiritual lives, it's our God-empowered persistence that keeps us moving forward.

About a year after my daughter, Lydia, was born, I fulfilled a lifelong dream of running a marathon. The twenty-six-plus miles were grueling, but five and a half hours after the starting gun went off, I crossed the finish line, exhausted. Often, when people learn that I ran a marathon, they ask, "How did you possibly run that far?" They can look at me and plainly see I am no super-athlete. First I say, "By the grace of God!" That usually gets a few laughs. Then I tell them the real secret, although it's really no secret at all: "I just kept putting one foot in front of the other."

There were times when I jogged along at a good pace. At other times I jogged slowly, and sometimes I walked. But it didn't matter whether I was jogging or walking; what mattered was that I continued to work my way toward the finish line. It wasn't speed that got me there, but persistence. In the same way, our Christian walk may sometimes feel more like a crawl. Through the toughest times in our spiritual lives, it's our God-empowered persistence that keeps us moving forward.

FOCUS ON JESUS. Besides throwing off things that hinder and running with perseverance, there's one last part of the Clarity Principle that we learn from Hebrews 12: "Let us fix our eyes on Jesus" (v. 2). Yes, the race can be grueling, but we don't have to run it alone. Jesus ran before us and is now at the finish line cheering us on. Not only is he our encourager, Jesus is also our role model.

In his thirty-three years on earth, Jesus provided the ultimate example of living simply in a complicated world. He was not status conscious or materialistic. He was certainly busy, yet he took time to rest and rejuvenate. Jesus knew his purpose in life and focused all of his energies in that direction. He proved it is possible to keep our hearts grounded when everything around us is topsy-turvy.

When Lydia was a tiny baby, she didn't warm up to others easily. Some infants will go to any friendly face, but Lydia wouldn't. Even her own grandparents couldn't hold her for more than just a few minutes before she protested loudly. Lydia was completely and totally focused on one thing: Mommy. I laugh now when I look back at pictures I took of her at only a few months old. Regardless of who was holding her, Lydia's eyes were always turned the other way—looking for Mommy.

Jesus proved it is possible to keep our hearts grounded when everything around us is topsy-turvy.

I was the one who gave her life (with a little help from Michael, of course), and I was the one who sustained her by feeding and caring for her. I was everything to her, so she didn't want to let me out of her sight. In the same way, Jesus is everything to us. He is the giver of life, he has redeemed our lives through his death on the cross, and he sustains our lives. How much simpler things would be if we adults stayed focused on Jesus as intently as baby Lydia stayed focused on me!

SIMPLIFYING from the INSIDE OUT

Applying the Clarity Principle allows you to successfully simplify your life from the inside out.

Right now, as you begin this book, you may not fully realize what is holding you back and causing the stress in your life. That's OK. In the chapters ahead, we'll unearth the root causes one by one. You will come to recognize these things for what they are—spiritual hindrances—and let them go. You will learn how to say good-bye and not look back.

Since the mind controls the body,

everything you do begins as a thought.

Next, you'll discover how to run the race with perseverance, how to keep your head in the game, how to avoid getting distracted by life's craziness and wandering off course. You'll learn how to keep moving forward even when progress is slow.

And finally, most importantly, you will come to see that the ultimate key is to keep your focus on Jesus. He *is* the way, and he will show you the way. As you deal with all the junk the world throws in your path, ask, "What would Jesus do?" That question is more than just a catchy slogan.

Throughout the rest of this book, we will apply the Clarity Principle to three distinct areas of life: our thoughts and attitudes, our time and possessions, and our money and resources.

We've already noted that in order to truly clarify life, we must work from the inside out. Therefore, we will discuss first what I call inner clarity, or simplicity of mind-set. Since the mind controls the body, everything you do begins as a thought. Simplifying this area of life means getting rid of any counterproductive thoughts that clutter your mind and wreak havoc in your life.

The next area we'll address is that of outer clarity, or simplicity of daily life. For our purposes, *daily life* is defined as your lifestyle—those things in your sphere of influence, in your corner of the world. Your lifestyle reflects what you believe and what you value most. The two aspects of lifestyle that usually need simplifying the most are how you use your time and how you relate to your possessions.

Simplifying the way you deal with time is a matter of learning to set boundaries and to align your schedule with your values. Simplifying how you handle possessions means learning to control how and when you acquire things and keeping a proper perspective on your belongings.

Your lifestyle reflects what you believe
and what you value most.

The final area we will explore is financial clarity, or simplicity of spending. Don't let the word *spending* fool you. We are not merely talking about how you spend your money, although that is certainly part of the equation. Financial clarity is more about how you relate to your money—do you own it or does it own you? Earning and spending money are inevitable facts of life, yet the attitude we harbor toward money is entirely up to us. Simplifying your financial life means learning to have the right attitude toward money and a healthy relationship with it.

Inner clarity, outer clarity, and financial clarity. We'll pursue all three together.

Several years ago I met a woman who shared how she has experienced these three types of simplifying. When Tina was younger, she was fully caught up in pursuing what she considered to be the good life. She enjoyed a luxurious home, closets full of expensive designer clothing, and weekly appointments to have her hair and nails done. Then something changed. "Slowly but surely," Tina says, "God began impressing upon my heart that I was wasting my time, my priorities, my resources, and my talents."

As God moved in her life, she saw that there was more to living than the constant pursuit of status and stuff. Over the course of a few years, Tina got rid of the big house, designer clothes, and standing appointment at the hair salon in favor of a modest home, minimal wardrobe, and a simple hairstyle she could maintain herself.

By outward appearances, Tina seemed to have gone from having it all to having close to nothing. In reality, these changes paved the way for a life that was better than she had ever known before. "I am richer by far because of my mental and spiritual joy than I ever was when I was burdened down by possessions, debt, and a corporate job where I felt only stress," Tina says. "I have everything I could ever possibly want—let alone need—and still God continues to heap blessings on me."

Tina's story illustrates the wonderful way in which the three areas of clarity overlap. Often if you begin working intently on one area, you will soon see changes in one or both of the other two areas. For example, suppose you suddenly lose your job and must cut your spending dramatically. This financial clarity leads to outer clarity—not acquiring more stuff to clutter up your home. Or maybe you experience a health crisis that forces you to trim your commitments to a bare minimum. Those steps toward outer clarity will cause you to reevaluate your priorities—inner clarity. This can then affect your spending—financial clarity is reached. Like an intricate jigsaw puzzle, these three areas fit together beautifully to give your life the clarity and continuity you desperately desire.

If you truly want to clarify, you have to start with the inside and work from there. Ready to get to work?

CLUTTER BUSTERS

◆ How does thinking of clutter as an internal condition with external symptoms affect your perspective on decluttering?

◆ Which of the three parts of the Clarity Principle will be the easiest for you to apply? Which will be the hardest? Who will you ask to help you move forward?

◆ Although Christians and non-Christians may take the same steps to live more simply, how might the motivation behind those actions differ?

COMING INTO CLARITY

I remember very well the breaking-point day—the day I realized something in my life had to change. I was working at a very stressful job at the time. That afternoon I was on my way to pick up my baby from day care. My knuckles were white because I was gripping the steering wheel so tightly. I was scowling, with my lips tight and deep lines on my forehead. The stress of my job was just too much.

That night I did some serious soul-searching. I didn't want to live any longer with so much stress and so little time for my family. I decided to quit my job. After that, I tried a couple of other jobs, but I always came back to my desire to be at home with my children. I sat down and figured our monthly expenses and our income. I was shocked to discover I had been working sixty hours a week to bring home only sixteen dollars after deducting all my work-related expenses— including gas, clothing, lunch, and after-school care for my youngest!

It seemed clear to my husband and me that the most obvious solution was for me to quit working. As we simplified our lifestyle, I discovered many ways to cut costs once I was at home. At year's end, we figured I'd "earned" half the salary I was supposedly making before, just in the savings I'd found!

Oddly, my family's physical health improved greatly. Our emotional relationships improved because we had time to actually listen and put our children and their needs first. Our marriage improved as I learned to trust that my husband will provide for this family, and he learned to trust that I will do my best to cover our needs with what he brings in. My walk with Christ has changed too. I find it easier to trust that our needs will be provided.

Terri
Reynolds, Georgia

from cluttered thoughts and attitudes to inner clarity

Since, then, you have been raised with Christ, set your hearts on things above, where Christ is seated at the right hand of God. Set your minds on things above, not on earthly things. For you died, and your life is now hidden with Christ in God.

Colossians 3:1-3

THREE

GOOD-BYE, CLUTTER!
Contentment is a choice I can make every day.

---

finding **contentment** in a *discontented* **world**

*I*f you and I were to meet in person, you'd know right away I'm from the South. I've lived practically my whole life in Tennessee. During my childhood my family took many trips to see relatives "back home" in Missouri, where both my parents grew up.

Our trips always included long drives down winding country roads, with weathered farmhouses, tiny country churches, and old family cemeteries often in view. But one of the things I enjoyed most about those trips was watching the cows silently scrutinize us as we drove by. Their curious faces told the whole story. They just couldn't figure out why we were invading their neck of the woods.

We always saw a few cows with their heads poked through the barbed wire fences, busily munching the grass on the other side. I found this baffling. As if all the grass on their side was not good enough, they risked getting cut and scraped by the barbs in order to reach the other side of the pasture. *Why do they do that?* I wondered. *Why go to so much trouble?* Why bother when the grass on their side was more than enough to satisfy their needs?

As I grew older, I began to comprehend the thing these bovines lived with—it's called discontentment. But cows aren't the only ones that have trouble being satisfied with where they are and what they have. We humans are also inclined to look past all the good things right in front of us. So many times we put our health, happiness, and sanity at risk as we reach for what seems better on the other side of the fence.

Have you ever thought, *I would be happy if only . . .* ? Do you often think about how much better life will be when your current state of affairs changes? Too often we're guilty of letting outer circumstances determine our inner level of contentment. The problem with this is that most of our outer circumstances are things over which we have very little control. If your contentment depends on your circumstances, you'll never be truly content because life's circumstances will never be completely perfect.

So many times we put our health, happiness,
and sanity at risk as we reach for what seems better
on the other side of the fence.

True contentment is not having everything you want, but learning to appreciate everything you have.

FREE to COUNT OUR BLESSINGS

Often we confuse being content with being happy or satisfied. Or worse, we think contentment is resigned acceptance of whatever comes our way. But true contentment goes much deeper.

Contentment is being able to come to terms with where you are and what's going on in your life, even if it's not what you would have chosen for yourself. Being content means being free to count your blessings and look for joy in your circumstances, whatever they may be.

When I think about what it means to be content, I think of my friend Judy. In the six years I've known her, Judy has gone through many challenges. For the last several years of their marriage, Judy's husband battled cancer and emphysema and suffered from depression. By the grace of God, Jim was able to continue working for most of that time, but his medical bills still created a financial strain.

Contentment is being able to come to terms with where you are and what's going on in your life, even if it's not what you would have chosen for yourself.

"If he ever gets too sick to work and loses his job, I don't know what we'd do," Judy often said during that time.

The stress of dealing with Jim's illness and being his primary caregiver took its toll on Judy, although she never complained. She was honest about her struggles, but never bitter or resentful. Through it all, Judy learned a great deal about contentment.

"I believe being content means being at peace with your circumstances," Judy told me once.

What a powerful statement! And what a powerful testimony coming from someone who faced extremely difficult circumstances. Was it fun for Judy to play the hand life dealt her?

Of course not. Would she have changed those circumstances if she could? Most definitely. Yet despite all her challenges, Judy was at peace. She could not control her circumstances, but she could control her responses to them. Judy chose to look to an eternal God rather than to fluctuating life conditions to find contentment.

Just like other unhealthy thoughts that litter our minds, discontentment is a form of clutter Satan uses to throw us off course. Our enemy loves luring us into this kind of inward focus so we won't have an upward focus. Life is filled with so many things we will never understand—things we were never meant to understand. Discontentment is counterproductive because it causes us to waste precious time and energy asking "Why?" in situations for which there are no answers.

THE SECRET of BEING CONTENT

The apostle Paul wrote a great deal about contentment, an issue that I believe was dear to his heart. Before he became a Christian, Paul was a man of power and influence, enjoying both the privileges of Roman citizenship and the authority of leadership in the Jewish community. For Paul, life was good.

Just like other unhealthy thoughts that litter our minds, discontentment is a form of clutter Satan uses to throw us off course.

Then everything changed. After he made a commitment to follow Christ, it wasn't long before Paul found himself spending a lot of time in prison. When he wasn't in jail, he was on the run from people who wanted him dead. He went without food, warm clothing, and other basic necessities. From a worldly standpoint, he went from prince to pauper.

Paul's secret was to rely not on his own abilities or willpower, but to look to God to give him the strength to be content even through the most difficult challenges.

Yet Paul wrote these famous words, found in Philippians 4:12, 13: "I have learned the secret of being content in any and every situation, whether well fed or hungry, whether living in plenty or in want. I can do everything through him who gives me strength." Paul's contentment was not based on externals. He put his hope in God, who never changes, rather than in circumstances, which do change from day to day. How did he do it? Paul's secret was to rely not on his own abilities or willpower, but to look to God to give him the strength to be content even through the most difficult challenges.

Don't misunderstand. I'm not talking about plastering a smile on your face and pretending everything is peaches and cream when it's not. Can my dear friend Faith make believe life is wonderful when mental illness has turned her world upside down? Even after years of treatment and brain surgery, her condition shows few signs of improvement. "God has helped me all the way," Faith says. "No matter how bad my illness gets, God never lets me give up, even when I say I want to."

Can my friend Colleen act as if nothing is wrong after a back injury ended her career? Five surgeries later, she still sees no prospect of returning to work. "It took about two and a half years," she says, "but I really feel much better with my situation, knowing that even if I don't bring home money, I contribute just by being Mom."

Being content clarifies life by keeping us focused on reality, not on the inevitable what-ifs and if-onlys.

Neither of these women would deny how challenging their circumstances have been. Yet both can attest that God has empowered them to find contentment as they rely on him.

Remember the Clarity Principle from chapter 2? A key part of that tells us to "run with perseverance the race marked out for us" (Hebrews 12:1). Contentment is a major component of that perseverance. It is easy to get distracted by things in life that aren't the way we would like them to be. Life isn't always fair; bad things do happen to good people. Yet being content clarifies life by keeping us focused on reality, not on the inevitable what-ifs and if-onlys. Contentment helps us keep pressing forward without stopping to dwell on life's lemons.

LIFE as I THOUGHT IT SHOULD BE

For many years, I was able to think of contentment only in terms of material possessions. During that time, if you asked me why people are not content, my automatic answer was, "Because they want more and more stuff without appreciating what they already have." Unfortunately, my canned response didn't bring me much comfort as I worked through my own issues with contentment.

I never struggled with wanting a larger home or fancier car or designer labels in my closet. My challenge was fretting over whether our lives would work out the way I thought they should. Michael and I both were raised with the belief that if you work hard, you will get ahead; yet that notion has not always been our experience. Our businesses grew slowly despite all our hard work. Michael studied for years to get a PhD but was not able to consistently find work in his area of specialization. We suffered several other setbacks beyond our control. On many occasions, I complained to God and begged to know why.

Michael and I both were raised with the belief that if you work hard, you will get ahead; yet that notion has not always been our experience.

In the same way, your contentment issues may have nothing to do with material possessions but rather with circumstances—challenging situations in life that haven't improved despite your best efforts. Although we hope and pray for healing from physical or mental illnesses or resolution for difficult conflicts, the reality is, these prayers are not always answered as we would wish. Contentment means running the race when things are going well—and continuing to run even when they are not.

No matter the source of your discontentment, understand three things:

CONTENTMENT IS WITHIN YOUR GRASP. Be encouraged. You can learn, as Paul did, to be at peace with your circumstances. Remember those cows? You must first stop sticking your head through the fence! Forget how green the grass appears somewhere else. By continually focusing on what is over there, you are unable to see the blessings of what's right here. In my situation, I needed to remind myself continually of the things that had gone right for us, rather than the things that had gone wrong.

CONTENTMENT THIEVES SHOULD BE ARRESTED. Pesky thought patterns rob you of your contentment and peace of mind. These thoughts start so innocently but can lead to major chaos. Something as harmless as admiring a friend's marriage, job, or financial situation can easily shift to comparing and finding inadequacy in your own marriage, work, or finances. The habit of dwelling on what-ifs can be equally dangerous. Lingering on what might have been only casts a dark shadow over what is.

The best way to deal with contentment thieves is to be aggressive in squelching this form of mental static. Refuse to allow your mind to wander down those paths. I've gone so far as to say an authoritative "No!" out loud to remind myself that these thoughts are not welcome.

THANKFULNESS CAN BE CULTIVATED. Contentment and thankfulness go hand in hand. The more thankful a person is, the more content she's likely to be. The less thankful a person is, the less content she's likely to be. Even if your circumstances aren't what you would consider ideal, choose to be thankful. And during the most trying times, you can certainly find something to be thankful for, even if it's just the knowledge that God is with you. You'll be amazed at how little you have to complain about when you spend a majority of your time giving thanks. Contentment grows as you nurture it with gratitude.

Lingering on what might have been only casts a dark shadow over what is.

So how is your level of contentment these days? Has discontentment cluttered your heart and confused your mind? If so, it doesn't have to be that way. Become a student of contentment. Learn to be content on the inside, no matter what's happening on the outside. Kiss the clutter of discontentment good-bye so you can welcome the clarity of being at peace with your circumstances.

CLUTTER *BUSTERS*

◆ When have you risked health, happiness, or sanity as you tried to pursue something beyond your grasp?

◆ What contentment thieves try to steal your peace of mind? What can you do now and in the future to put those thieves under lock and key?

◆ What is the biggest challenge you are facing right now? Close your eyes and imagine being able to say, as Paul did, "I have learned the secret of being content in any and every situation." What's the first step you will take toward contentment despite this challenge?

COMING INTO CLARITY

My childhood was split by the divorce and remarriage of both my parents. I heard so much discontentment from all sides, even from my stepparents. I found myself drawn into reading—romance, biographies, self-help—to escape this constant barrage. I read all about other people's lives in an attempt to get away from my own—anything to escape my world.

In doing this, I began to want the lifestyles in these books. I longed for fairytale endings in which the knight in shining armor rides up on his trusty steed (as my husband did—except his horse was a silver Cougar XR7) and rescues the damsel in distress (as my husband did—the damsel was me). But unlike the fairy tales where the knight and damsel live happily ever after, my husband and I were never happy all the time. Before I knew it, my life became a repeat of what I'd heard my whole life! I was parroting the same kind of discontentment I'd heard from my parents—until I realized it wasn't getting me anywhere.

After that realization, I recommitted myself to the Lord and began to seek him earnestly. Life was so difficult then, as my husband and I had many differences. But with God's help, we began learning this lifestyle of contentment together. It has not been easy, but recently we celebrated twenty-eight years of marriage. No matter what life brings to our door, we can rest assured that God knew it was coming before it even began its path there—and he will help us through it.

Patti
Waterloo, Indiana

44

FOUR

GOOD-BYE, CLUTTER!
I'm fed up with pursuing what the world offers. Those things don't satisfy like I thought they would!

satisfaction guaranteed

During my junior year of college, I worked a crazy 2:00 AM to 9:00 AM shift and took a full load of classes. Because my work and school hours were scattered throughout the day and night, getting more than four or five hours of sleep at a time was impossible. To complicate things even more, I lived an hour from campus, making it impractical to run home between classes. Fortunately, my parents lived near the college, so I often used their guest room when I needed to crash.

Spring semester that year was particularly grueling. In addition to the morning and evening classes I had on other days, on Thursdays I had morning, afternoon, and evening classes. This meant that on Thursdays I worked from 2:00 AM to 9:00 AM, went to classes all day and evening, raced back to my parents' house for a couple hours of sleep, and then went back to work early Friday morning for another seven-hour shift. By the time I could finally go home and hit the bed, I had been in motion for more than thirty hours with little more than a catnap.

Friday mornings at work were pure torture. During those shifts, which seemed to last forever, I noticed something unusual. When my body needed sleep so desperately, it compensated for the lack of fulfillment of that need by crying out for gratification in other areas. At times when I wasn't hungry, I craved food as if I were famished. I longed for liquids when I wasn't thirsty. My skin crawled, even though it had no legitimate reason to itch. It was as if my body was saying, "If you won't give me what I really need, I'll demand something else!"

We find no genuine satisfaction until we give our hearts and spirits what they need.

Ironically, although I ate and drank and scratched, none of these was satisfying. My body needed one thing and one thing only—sleep—and it wouldn't be satisfied until that need was met.

Just as God designed our physical bodies to require sleep, he also created our spirits to crave things only he can provide. Something inside us longs to experience all that a close relationship with him brings. But we often short-circuit God's plans by trying to fulfill emotional and spiritual needs in other ways. The end result is always the same: we find no genuine satisfaction until we give our hearts and spirits what they need.

UNSATISFYING SUBSTITUTES

Have you ever wondered why things you used to enjoy don't bring the pleasure they once did? Have you ever been disappointed when a new purchase didn't make you happy like you thought it would? Do you sometimes find yourself making purchase after purchase because each one seems to fall short of your expectations? Often we fall into the trap of thinking material possessions can bring lasting fulfillment. Somehow we think *things* will scratch that inner itch or stop our emotional tummies from rumbling.

The truth is that when you try to fill spiritual needs with worldly things, you soon learn that the satisfaction is short-lived. Have you ever tried to use the wrong tool for a job? I remember once trying to use a large regular screwdriver to remove a small Phillips-head screw. By trying to force the regular screwdriver to work, I stripped the grooves on the head of the screw, making it nearly impossible to remove. Our spiritual and emotional needs work the same way. God uniquely designed us in such a manner that only one thing—himself—will fill the voids he purposely created in us. No other tool will get the job done.

Somehow we think things *will scratch that inner itch or stop our emotional tummies from rumbling.*

Yvonne is a friend of mine who learned this lesson firsthand. Within the span of one week, she suffered three crushing blows: she was downsized from her job, she learned that her dad had cancer, and her husband told her he wanted a divorce.

"My whole life was ripped out from under me," Yvonne remembers. "For several months after that, I spent money like it was going out of style."

Yvonne didn't buy anything but necessities, such as pantyhose for work, health and beauty products she used regularly, and household items. But the quantities in which she purchased these things were astounding: forty pairs of pantyhose, fifteen bottles of contact lens solution, twelve boxes of dishwasher detergent . . . She was trying to stock up on things she needed as a way of compensating for the sense of security she had lost.

Why wait on God's timing when satisfaction is only a quick shopping trip or Internet order away?

"Through counseling, I realized I needed to come back to God. I had been away from him for about fifteen years," she says. "That was what I really needed—security I couldn't buy in a store."

The notion that things can somehow meet our needs is simply another strand in Satan's web of deception. This hoax is clutter, as are many of the other lies Satan uses to entangle and entrap us. Because possessions can be seen, touched, and handled, it is all too easy to look to them for comfort and relief from whatever ails us. A new purchase can be a quick fix to ease those inner longings. And because we can control the influx of possessions into our lives, we are lured into thinking we are self-sufficient. Why wait on God's timing when satisfaction is only a quick shopping trip or Internet order away?

EMPTY CALORIES

I confess I am a bit of a junk food junkie. When faced with the choice of fresh fruit or a handful of chocolate chip cookies, I'll take the cookies every time. Within an otherwise balanced diet, I know there is nothing wrong with enjoying a few sweets here and there, but it's up to me to make sure cookies don't replace the healthy foods my body needs. In the same way, when God gives us material possessions and experiences to enjoy, he wants us to derive pleasure from them, but he doesn't want that pleasure to take the place of the spiritual and emotional sustenance only he can provide.

The Bible warns us about the dangers of looking to temporary diversions to satisfy deep-seated needs. Isaiah 55:2 asks bluntly, "Why spend money on what is not bread, and your labor on what does not satisfy? Listen, listen to me, and eat what is good, and your soul will delight in the richest of fare." Why waste time and money gorging yourself on empty calories that will never fill you up? Why run yourself ragged chasing after frivolous things that fade away? God is our only true source of satisfaction. Compared to what he offers us, everything else is junk food—empty calories.

A friend shared with me how she first began to see the difference between finding fulfillment in worldly things and finding true fulfillment in a relationship with God. Before Penny and her husband became Christians, they and their three children were invited to dinner at the home of a lower-income family they had recently met.

The Bible warns us about the dangers of looking to temporary diversions to satisfy deep-seated needs.

This family's house was tiny, with bare concrete floors and worn furniture. That night everyone in the family was excited because they were having a special treat: ice cream for dessert. Because money was tight, ice cream was a rarity.

"I remember thinking that we had ice cream in our freezer every day. We could have it anytime we wanted," Penny recalls.

Yet there was something this family had that Penny's family didn't. "We could feel the peace and joy in that house. I wanted it for my family too."

Remember the first part of the Clarity Principle we found in Hebrews 12? "Let us throw off everything that hinders" (v. 1). The fallacy that material things fulfill us is a hindrance to many women. It creeps in subtly, partially because it is deeply ingrained in our culture's concept of what it means to live well. From an early age, we are taught to chase the American Dream and all that goes with it. Sadly, this delusion complicates our lives by keeping us spiritually undernourished.

Life becomes much more clear when you understand that *things* can never satisfy the deep longings of the heart. When you grasp this truth, you are freed from the constant drive for instant gratification. You are free to enjoy possessions without being controlled by them, because you know they cannot meet all your needs.

Filling Up on the Best

The tendency to look to things to fill us up can manifest itself in unexpected ways. I realized this a few years ago when I began to see an unhealthy pattern developing in my life.

Anyone who knows me well knows that I am a garage-sale aficionada. Every Saturday morning from early spring until late fall, my family hits the streets in search of sales. I love finding an inexpensive skirt or blazer or anything else to add to my wardrobe. Although there's nothing wrong with enjoying a good deal, the problem is that even buying things inexpensively can become addictive. There's almost a high that comes from getting something new each week, wearing a different outfit to church each Sunday, and having a constant flow of new additions to my wardrobe.

I knew it probably wasn't healthy to be so fascinated with my bargain shopping, but then something happened that confirmed my suspicion. One Saturday without any great bargains turned into two. Then two turned into three, three into four . . . and next thing I knew, I had gone through a whole yard-sale season without any real treasures. It didn't take a degree in rocket science to sense that maybe God was trying to tell me something. Maybe I had become just a little too dependent on my yard-sale habit. Rather than waiting for his provision, I was looking to my next bargain for my next thrill. See what I mean about this attitude sneaking in subtly?

Ask God to show you ways in which you regularly look to sources other than him for fulfillment. When you ask, be ready to be surprised at what he may reveal!

So how do you switch your focus from finding satisfaction in worldly stuff to finding satisfaction in God? Consider these three steps that will help you:

RECOGNIZE THAT THERE IS A PROBLEM. Things God gives us to enjoy can easily stand in the way of our enjoying God. Have you allowed yourself to be so filled up on junk food that you don't have room left for God's feast? If you're not sure, ask God to show you ways in which you regularly look to sources other than him for fulfillment. When you ask, be ready to be surprised at what he may reveal! I never would have thought my yard-sale hobby could become a problem. Likewise, you may realize that some other seemingly harmless habit isn't as harmless as you thought.

RELEASE THAT PROBLEM TO GOD. Once you have identified problem areas, invite God into the situation to help you change. Ask him to suppress your appetite for quick fixes and temporary highs and to replace it with a healthy hunger for the lasting satisfaction only he can give. In addition to asking for his help, do your part by positioning yourself to better connect with him. Spend some extra time in prayer. Listen to praise and worship music. Participate in a new Bible study. These activities will help you draw near to God so you can experience fulfillment in him.

RUN FROM PROBLEMS BEFORE THEY START. Make a commitment to avoid those situations in which you are tempted to seek temporary gratification. For me, this meant limiting my yard-sale purchases to items I truly needed. If your downfall is shopping at the mall, go only when you have a legitimate need. If you are a sucker for mail-order catalogs, don't even open them before throwing them away. If you look to entertainment for your feel-goods, restrict the frequency of your restaurant or movie outings. Break the control these hindrances have over you by controlling your contact with them.

If you look to entertainment for your feel-goods, restrict the frequency of your restaurant or movie outings.

Have you been trying to find lasting happiness in temporary pleasures? If so, you are eating a greasy burger and fries when you could be dining on lobster and prime rib! But as you learn to depend less and less on things, you will find the clarity of satisfaction like you've never known before.

CLUTTER *BUSTERS*

◆ When have you realized that something seemingly benign was really a hindrance in disguise?

◆ What are some examples of "empty calories" in your life—things that may temporarily fill you up but don't meet your deepest needs?

◆ Isaiah 55:2 compares the satisfaction we get from God and his love to the experience of eating the finest of foods. When have you experienced God's love in that way?

COMING INTO CLARITY

Recently we sold a large home and bought one much smaller. Our new home used a different color scheme than my previous home, so I faced a choice: either I could spend a huge amount of money to redecorate, or I could use the things I already had and adapt them to the colors in the new house.

I really struggled with what to do. I was tempted to buy a lot of new things, but I finally thought, 'Why? I'm fifty-two years old. I could be gone in a year or ten years. I love the things I already own. New things won't make me love the house any more than I already do, and new furnishings won't make my new house a home.

So I adapted. I found I could use a lot of things I already owned in new ways. I gained a new perspective on buying things. When many people have so much less than I do, why spend money on new things that I don't really need? God is good and gives me just what I need.

Melodie
Elizabethtown, Pennsylvania

FIVE

GOOD-BYE, CLUTTER!
*It's time for worry and me to go our separate ways. I'm trading
that imposter in for a bigger, better model called trust.*

---

the secret of a worry-free life

A few months after Michael and I were married, we purchased our first home. With three bedrooms, two full baths, a roomy kitchen, and two-car garage, the house had everything we wanted. But it also came equipped with something we didn't want: a home security system.

We agreed we wouldn't bother taking the system out, but we didn't plan to use it either. The neighborhood seemed safe enough; why go to the trouble and expense of a monitored security system? So because we didn't plan to activate the system, we thought we didn't need to bother learning how to use it either.

Just a few weeks after we moved in, early one Sunday morning before church, Michael was in one bathroom taking a shower, and I was in the other doing the same thing. Suddenly our alarm siren began screeching loud enough for the whole neighborhood to hear.

Stunned, Michael and I both jumped out of our showers and stood, naked and dripping wet, wondering what in the world was going on. Was someone breaking into our home? Would the police be there any minute? And most of all, how could we make the alarm stop?

"Michael, what should we do?" I shrieked. "What should we do?!"

In his usual matter-of-fact way, Michael said firmly, "Put our clothes on."

Running around like headless chickens would get us nowhere. And if the police did arrive, going to the door without a stitch of clothing on was not a good idea! Rather than wasting time worrying about all the unknowns—what set off the alarm, what to do to make it stop—we needed to stay focused on what we *did* know and what we could reasonably do to deal with the problem at hand.

The police did not show up that day. We finally quieted the alarm by flipping the circuit breaker in the garage, and later Michael permanently fixed the problem by cutting all the wires connected to the system's control box. We never did learn how to use that alarm, but we never had another problem with it either.

WORRY, the ULTIMATE FREELOADER

I learned something about worry that day. Often when problems come, we run around wasting time and energy reacting rather than concentrating on what we can logically do to deal with the situation. Rather than preparing ourselves for action, we stand there naked and dripping, shrieking, "What should we do? What should we do?!"

How much time do you spend each day fretting about things over which you have no control? And even with those things you *can* control, do you often worry whether your best efforts are good enough? Worry is the ultimate freeloader. It takes so much out of us yet gives back nothing in return. Not only is worry unproductive, it's actually counterproductive because it drives us to do the opposite of what we need to do. Worry causes us to focus on ourselves—what we can do to fix the situation— rather than on God and his infinite ability to handle whatever challenges come our way.

Are you a worrier? My friend Faith is. Or at least that's what her husband, Mark, told us once. "I don't have to worry," he joked. "Faith does enough of it for both of us!"

Worry is the ultimate freeloader. It takes so much out of us yet gives back nothing in return.

Mark was teasing, but for some women, worry truly is a way of life. Others consider worry to be just an annoying habit or an inevitable part of being a woman. But don't be deceived—there is much more to worrying than that. Worry is another one of the weapons in our enemy's arsenal, and he uses it skillfully against us. As women, we are wired to crave security and stability. When life feels neither stable nor secure, worry is often our first course of action.

When faced with any sort of worrisome situation, it is not uncommon to feel bombarded by uncertainty and confusion. These feelings are natural, but they are also the enemy's ace. By keeping your mind and energy focused on what you don't and can't know, Satan keeps your attention away from what is certain: the truth about God and his everlasting goodness.

Like all other forms of clutter, worry stands in the way of clarity. Unfortunately, it doesn't travel alone. Worry hangs out with a whole gang of other unsavory characters. Have you ever noticed how worrying can lead to distrust—thinking less than the best of yourself, others, and God? Discouragement often tags along too, tempting you to give up when you should keep moving forward. Other hitchhikers include regret and even ingratitude. Any and all of these will try to hop on board when you give worry a ride.

THE SECRET of a WORRY-FREE LIFE

Do you want to see a perfect example of what it means to live worry free? Just look at a tiny baby nursing contentedly at his mother's breast. That baby isn't concerned about what's going on around him. He isn't distracted by questions—*What if this happens?* or *What will I do about that?* All he knows is that Mommy has things under control and she's taking care of him. All kinds of craziness could be happening right outside his nursery window, but the little one won't even flinch as long as he is nestled safely in his mother's arms.

Worry hangs out with a whole gang of
other unsavory characters.

The life of an infant is fairly straightforward: eat, sleep, and cry when it's time for a clean diaper. As adults, our lives are a little more complex: family, career, relationships, health issues, financial concerns . . . Yet we can still rest in childlike serenity. Our Father has things under control, and he's taking care of us. When life seems to be breaking down around us, we can face our struggles without flinching because our Father holds us close.

Jesus said, "Who of you by worrying can add a single hour to his life? Since you cannot do this very little thing, why do you worry about the rest?" (Luke 12:25, 26). Choosing not to worry is simply turning over any pretense of being in control to the one who truly is. Letting go of worry actually addresses two aspects of the Clarity Principle in Hebrews 12:1, 2: "Let us throw off everything that hinders" and "Let us fix our eyes on Jesus." Worry is a physical, emotional, and spiritual hindrance, but you can beat it if you learn to look to your heavenly Father and his Son, Jesus, when problems and uncertainty come your way. Life becomes much simpler when you focus on what you know—that God is more than able to handle things—rather than on what you don't know.

My friend Connie has a humorous testimony of a time when God taught her a lesson about worry. Connie lives in the Gulf Shores area of Alabama, where Hurricane Ivan hit in 2004. When Ivan hit, a foot of water and mud damaged items in the carport and storage area under Connie's house, and the high wind damaged the patio doors and pulled shingles off several areas of the roof.

Life becomes much simpler when you focus on what you know—that God is more than able to handle things— rather than on what you don't know.

A contractor had been remodeling Connie's home even before the hurricane hit. He had committed to fixing any hurricane damage, but he didn't make good on his promise. By the time Connie realized she couldn't depend on him, ten days had passed, and all the roofers in the area had waiting lists of three to four months. As a single woman caring for her elderly mom, Connie was sick with worry.

"Finally," Connie said, "I just prayed, 'God, you have to find me a roofer. I can't worry about this anymore!' Immediately I felt a calm peacefulness surround me."

That calm didn't last long though. Just a couple of hours later, Connie's mother discovered that a water pipe had burst. Now Connie needed a roofer *and* a plumber! As she called the first business in the phone book that did emergency plumbing repairs, she wondered why God wasn't helping her more.

This contractor showed up the next morning and repaired the plumbing problem for a reasonable price. As he was leaving, he casually asked if she wanted him to give her a quote on fixing her roof too. Two days later, her roof was fixed, and Connie asked the contractor to complete several more jobs around her house.

One year later, Connie ended up marrying the contractor!

"I tell people he was cheaper to buy than to rent," Connie jokes. "He tells people he was waiting until he got my house just the way he wanted it. God definitely takes away your worry—even though he sometimes answers your prayers in ways you don't expect. Only *he* would repair my roof by breaking my water pipe!"

SAY GOOD-BYE to WORRY for GOOD

From day one of kindergarten, my daughter, Lydia, excelled in all areas except one: handwriting. Counting from one to thirty? Check. Days of the week? Check. Consonant sounds? Check. Handwriting? Disaster. Lydia's fine motor skills were not fully developed, and no matter how much I begged, bribed, or scolded, her printing showed little improvement.

Being an uptight and overprotective parent, I talked to her teacher about this. I talked to other parents. I talked to Michael. I talked to God about it too, but not as much as I should have.

In hindsight, I can see that I should have turned the matter over to God and trusted that Lydia would form this skill when she was developmentally ready, without my being a drill sergeant. I should have, but I didn't. I let my worry drive me to try to fix the situation. Consequently, Lydia and I endured many tense sessions of my trying to somehow squeeze neat penmanship out of her. As I look back on the situation now, I see the needless stress I caused by not being able to relinquish my worry.

Have you ever been in a similar situation? Do you often find yourself walking in worry instead of trusting in the one who has everything under control? If so, here are three strategies that helped me finally get worry under control:

FIND A LISTENING EAR. Find a friend who will listen objectively as you describe what is worrying you. Worry often loses its power when you put it into words. Things that seem big and bad in your own mind become much more manageable when you describe them to someone who is not so emotionally involved.

EXAMINE THE PROBLEM OBJECTIVELY. Analyze your worrisome situation with this question in mind: How much of this is really under my control? One giant step toward snuffing out worry is to acknowledge that a great deal of what happens in life is beyond your control. Once you see what you can and cannot control in the situation, decide on a positive plan of action for those things you can change. Then make a rigid commitment to let go of those things you cannot change.

GUARD YOUR MIND AGAINST WORRY. Be aggressive in not allowing your mind to wander down the path of worry. Just like contentment thieves, thoughts of worry can sneak in when you don't expect them. These thoughts can quickly and easily shatter your trust and steal your peace of mind. When worry tries to sneak back in after you've let it go, be ruthless. Stop worry dead in its tracks by replacing thoughts of worry with thoughts of trust.

When worry tries to sneak back in after you've let it go, be ruthless. Stop worry dead in its tracks.

Are you ready to live a worry-free life? Has worry held you down and held you back long enough? Give up trying to manage and manipulate. Choose instead to embrace the simplicity of knowing your Father has everything under control. When you do, clarity will come closer than you ever thought possible.

CLUTTER *BUSTERS*

◆ Why do you think God sometimes chooses to answer our prayers in unusual ways, as he did in Connie's situation?

◆ Do you agree that worry is the ultimate freeloader because it takes much more than it gives in return? What are some examples of things worry has taken from you?

◆ Is it is easier for you to relinquish major problems or minor problems into God's care? Why is this true?

COMING INTO CLARITY

This year my family has gone through a very difficult challenge involving a legal battle over a house we were renting with an option to buy. When we moved into the house, it was falling apart. We started fixing it up and making repairs because we knew we were going to buy it eventually. But when the time came for us to purchase the home, one of the owners changed her mind. She wanted to kick us out immediately.

The owner finally decided she could not win because we had a contract. But the legal costs of this four-month battle were about four thousand dollars, not to mention the stress and strain on my family. During this ordeal, I was waking up in the middle of the night and crying and praying to God for mercy. Finally, one day I surrendered the situation completely to him. "I don't have anything left to fall back on," I told him.

Soon after that, things began to turn around. Through this experience, I realized that when things seem to fall apart, God wants us to turn to him as our resource. I used to always have a Plan B. He finally got through to me that he is my Plan A and Plan B. He showed me that the most important contract to have is the one we have with him, a binding covenant that says, "Never will I leave you; never will I forsake you" (Hebrews 13:5).

Sherry
Crawfordville, Florida

SIX

GOOD-BYE, CLUTTER!
I'm ready to place my confidence in what will never let me down.

---

letting go of the untrustables

I've never met a bread I didn't like. Rolls, biscuits, bagels, muffins, croissants—of all the food groups, the grains group is by far my favorite! Not only do I love eating bread, I enjoy making it as well. I often use my bread machine to whip up something special, especially when we are having company. Nothing entices dinner guests like the irresistible aroma of fresh bread wafting from my kitchen.

Not long ago, when company was coming, I flipped through one of my cookbooks and decided to make a batch of herbed monkey bread. I pulled the baking pan from the bread machine and positioned it and my cookbook on the counter so I could easily follow the recipe. Water, olive oil, sugar, salt . . . One by one I placed each ingredient into the pan. Oregano, garlic, black pepper, basil . . . *Garlic? Black pepper? Basil?* Something was wrong.

To my surprise, my cookbook was open to an herb rolls recipe, not herbed monkey bread. Somehow the book's pages had flipped to the rolls recipe on the next page, maybe stirred by a breeze drifting in through the open kitchen window.

What to do, what to do? I thought.

I quickly compared the ingredients I had already added with the ingredients I should have added. Maybe I could recover from this mishap by simply making minor adjustments to the rest of the recipe.

How often we put our trust in things that are not trustworthy and rely on things that are not truly reliable!

You wouldn't think a little garlic, black pepper, and basil would have made that much difference, but believe me, they did. Rather than being light, fluffy, and golden brown, the bread was dense, with a strange texture and flavor. Instead of raving over my homemade bread and quickly going for seconds, my guests barely touched it. I ended up throwing most of it out for the birds the next day. Poor things.

SEARCHING for SECURITY

Aren't we often guilty of putting our confidence in things that can shift with the slightest wind of change? Think about the components of your life that you tend to look to for security. How often we put our trust in things that are not trustworthy and rely on things that are not truly reliable!

Do you feel a sense of security because you enjoy good health and gratifying relationships? Does your future seem bright because you've made steady progress up the corporate ladder? Do you take comfort in the size of your investment portfolio?

Career advancement, physical fitness, satisfying relationships, good financial health—these are all admirable goals, but the temptation is great to trust these temporal things.

Companies fold. Investments disappoint. Friendships end. The illusion of good health vanishes with one phone call from the doctor. In our ever-changing world, life fluctuates from minute to minute. Only God and his love for us remain the same. Trust is a limited commodity. Every bit that we place in other things leaves us with less to place in God and his unchangeable goodness and mercy.

THE TRAP of MISPLACED TRUST

Have you ever noticed how kids have an insatiable appetite for exploring the world around them? If there's anything new or interesting to investigate, you can be sure your children will check it out. God made them that way. This drive to explore and experience everything in their environment is healthy because it enables kids to grow and learn, but it does have its downside. Because of their unquenchable curiosity, children often put themselves into dangerous situations. How many trips to the emergency room result from a kid's need to "know" overriding any semblance of common sense?

Trust is a limited commodity. Every bit that we place in other things leaves us with less to place in God and his unchangeable goodness and mercy.

Just as God made children with a strong curiosity, God made women with a strong craving for security. We want to feel safe and to know that everything will be all right. This need for solidity has its good points. Without it we probably wouldn't work as hard as we do to create a stable home environment for our families. But it can also cause problems. Satan uses this need for constancy against us by tempting us to put our trust in things that by nature are not as constant as we might think. Promising careers, financial assets, good health, and yes, even the relationships we hold dear can all fail. These things can and will let us down when we look to them for our sense of welfare.

God's Word reminds us of the foolishness of putting our faith in things that can be here today, gone tomorrow: "What do you know about tomorrow? How can you be so sure about your life? It is nothing more than mist that appears for only a little while before it disappears" (James 4:14, *CEV*). The things in life that we can touch and see and feel and manipulate are the very things that pass away. Trusting in these transient elements complicates life by giving us an unrealistic and unhealthy sense of security. This kind of heart clutter distorts our vision and distracts our focus away from our only true source of security.

The things in life that we can touch and see and feel and manipulate are the very things that pass away.

A friend of mine once shared how God had impressed this truth upon her. When Kathy was in her twenties, she had an ideal of what she thought a happy and satisfying life would be. Her mental picture included a house with a white picket fence, nice cars, a wonderful husband, and perfect children. These are the things she believed would bring security and fulfillment to her life. Unfortunately, life did not work out according to her plans.

"When I was in my thirties, I became aware that my timetable for these things was lagging behind," Kathy says. "Then just as I reached my forties, my marriage of twenty-four years came to an end."

After her divorce, Kathy was left with little income and two children to raise by herself. During this time, she learned some hard lessons about being content and trusting God when other things in life failed her. Instead of looking to a happy marriage or a comfortable financial situation for security, she learned to look to God.

Trusting in God alone puts into practice the second element of the Clarity Principle.

"Bad times will pass. Good times will pass too, but our Lord and his peace are with us always," Kathy says. "Now, in my fifties, I don't have the material things I once felt were so important, but I enjoy each day as it comes and serve the Lord with gladness."

Trusting in God alone puts into practice the second element of the Clarity Principle: "Let us run with perseverance the race marked out for us." Letting go of misplaced trust is freeing; it empowers you to deal with the challenges of life effectively. When you do lose a job or suffer financial setbacks, it doesn't completely rock your world. Even in major crises such as disability or divorce, you can face the challenges with resolve. In the midst of trouble, you can be like a tree planted beside a raging river. You can be immovable, not because of your own inner strength or fortitude, but because your roots go deep— straight to the one who never lets you down.

DADDY WILL BE BACK

My older sister, whose name is also Kathy, was seven years old when I was born. Kathy and my dad were both wildly excited about having a new baby in the family, and Kathy went to the hospital with my dad on the day I was to come home. Children weren't allowed in the maternity ward in those days, so Dad left Kathy in the waiting room, telling her not to go anywhere and that he'd be back soon with Mom and me.

After my mother and I were discharged, Dad wheeled us out to the car. It wasn't until they were about to pull out of the parking lot that Mom noticed something was wrong.

"Bill, where's Kathy?" she asked.

Red-faced, Dad rushed back inside the hospital to get my sister. In all the hubbub, he had completely forgotten about Kathy in the waiting room. When he found her, she was still sitting patiently in the same spot where he had left her. She wasn't crying or fretting—just waiting as he'd told her to do.

What makes this story remarkable is that Kathy actually saw Dad leave with Mom and me; the waiting room was right next to hospital entrance. She had watched him wheel Mom and me past her without so much as a glance her way—but she wasn't worried. Dad had said he would be back to get her, and she believed him. Even though it appeared the family was leaving without her, she trusted that Dad knew what he was doing.

I think about this story as I recall times when I have been tempted to shift my trust from the infinite God to the temporary things of life. Life is much less cluttered and complicated when I place my trust in my heavenly Father as completely as Kathy trusted our earthly father that day.

Are there things you look to for security that could easily let you down? If so, here are some steps to help you learn to take the trust you've placed in transient things and give it to the one who is completely trustworthy.

Talk to your Father about situations that test your ability to trust him fully.

INSULATE YOURSELF BY STAYING GROUNDED IN GOD'S WORD. Like God himself, his Word does not change. If you are going to put your trust in him, you need to know who he is and what he is all about. What better way to do that than to read his love letter to you? Just as you eat every day to keep your body well fed, make it a priority to spend time in God's Word each day to feed your spirit as well.

EDUCATE YOURSELF BY MEMORIZING TRUST-BUILDING PASSAGES. In addition to reading God's Word, invest time and effort in memorizing portions that remind you of God's faithfulness and dependability. Find verses that apply to your unique situation and commit them to memory. By memorizing your own special Scriptures, you will always have them handy when you need the encouragement they provide.

ALIGN YOURSELF BY CONNECTING TO GOD THROUGH PRAYER. Confess that you are guilty of placing your trust in places where it doesn't belong. Ask for God's help in giving that trust back to him. Talk to your Father about situations that test your ability to trust him fully. You wouldn't go for several days without speaking to your family or others you live with, would you? Then why go for several days without speaking to God?

What's holding you back in this area of trust? Do you see ways in which misplaced trust has distracted you from trusting fully in God? If so, you are missing out on trust that will never let you down. Give this hindrance its walking papers so you can rest in the security—and clarity—only God can provide.

◆ CLUTTER *BUSTERS* ◆

- ◆ What parts of your life do you tend to look to for security? Your job? Marriage or family relationships? Health or physical appearance? Finances? What is the difference between a healthy confidence in these things and an unhealthy trust?

- ◆ Kathy maintained her trust even though it looked as if her dad had left her at the hospital. Are you able to have that same kind of trust in God, even when you don't understand what's happening in your life?

- ◆ What situations have tested your ability to trust God fully? How did God reveal more of his nature to you through those situations?

- ◆ In what situations today are you having trouble trusting God? What is it about those that make trust more difficult for you? What has God taught you in the past that you can lean on now?

COMING INTO CLARITY

As a woman, my greatest joy is relationships. However, as a home-schooled teenager in a bad neighborhood and a small church, I had no friends. When I was a grown woman, my best friend dumped me because she thought I wasn't being sensitive enough to her need for my time. Other friendships have failed too. I've cried out to God for a few close women friends, but my relationships usually continue to disappoint.

This has been hard for me through the years, but now at the age of forty, I no longer feel the tremendous insecurity I used to feel over a lack of close friends. God has provided me with a few ladies to whom I relate well. While these relationships are not exactly what I long for, I can now see that many times God wants us to cry out to him and trust him in the areas of our lives that disappoint us the most.

In this case, he has taught me that he is the only friend that will never fail us, and that each of us also fails at being a friend at times, even though we may not mean to. This failure is often exactly what we need to help us see how incredibly trustworthy he is.

Rachel
Hudsonville, Michigan

SEVEN

GOOD-BYE, CLUTTER!
*I've had enough of a faulty self-image! Now I'm getting
a God's-eye view, and I like what I see.*

---

seeing ourselves as God *sees* us

When Lydia was three, she attended the preschool at our church several mornings a week. Being the social child that she is, she loved interacting with her teachers and playing with all her friends. Lydia became particularly close to a few of the little girls in her class, and at Christmastime she wanted to make gifts for them.

After much discussion, we decided to make tree ornaments, using a craft kit from her grandmother. I knew I would have to help because the ornaments required assembling some small parts. What I didn't know was that Lydia would be bored after only thirty seconds and I would end up making all the ornaments myself!

A few days after the gifts had been distributed, the mother of one of Lydia's friends stopped me in the preschool hallway and told me how impressed she was with the beautiful ornaments Lydia made.

"There must be something wrong with *my* kids," she added. "None of them could ever put together something like that at age three!"

I quickly assured her there was nothing wrong with her kids— Lydia couldn't do it either!

Although the gifts were Lydia's idea and she chose the patterns and colors, she couldn't take credit for making them; it was Mommy who did all the work. Lydia wanted to do something nice for her friends and thought she could make the ornaments herself, but despite her good intentions she was helpless to pull it off without my help.

Do you feel confident that you can breeze through life with little more than a divine nod from above?

Aren't we adults like that sometimes? We live in an individualistic society that values self-reliance and taking charge of one's own destiny. We'd rather not think of ourselves as being dependent upon anyone. We take great pride in saying "I did it myself" without acknowledging how much we rely on God. Children aren't the only ones who often overestimate their ability to be self-sufficient.

GOD LOVES ME, but DOES HE LIKE ME?

Often we intellectually admit that we need God, but practically we choose to go it alone. Is your image of yourself overinflated? Do you take pride in making your own way? Do you feel confident that you can breeze through life with little more than a divine nod from above?

Or maybe you underinflate your self-image. Have people put you down or done things that caused you to feel worthless? Do you recognize your need for God but wonder whether he's really willing to help? Is it hard for you to believe that God likes you, much less loves you?

We are valuable because of who God made us to be and what he can do through us.

Underrating yourself can be just as dangerous as overrating. These two viewpoints are on opposite ends of the spectrum, but both are miles from the truth. We are not self-sufficient beings with little need for God. We are dependent on God for everything—even our sense of self-worth. And we are precious to God. As part of God's magnificent creation and made in his image, you are more valuable to him than you'll ever know.

We are not the scum of the earth, but we're not the center of the universe either. God created us for his plans. Our value comes not from who we are or what we can do. We are valuable because of who God made us to be and what he can do through us.

Ugly Betty

The TV show *Ugly Betty,* starring America Ferrera as Betty Suarez, debuted in the fall of 2006. It quickly became a hit. Betty is a slightly plump, plain Jane hired as assistant to the new editor of a fashion magazine. Although Betty has both personality and brains, her sense of style and confidence in her looks has not kept pace.

A couple of years ago, I was chatting with a group of women at church when someone suggested taking a group picture. At the very word *photograph,* one of the ladies—whose name was, believe it or not, Betty—began to protest vehemently. Although everyone else was excited about having our picture taken together, Betty made it perfectly clear she would not participate. The rest of us tried to persuade her, but Betty stood firm.

"You don't understand," she answered. "I wouldn't even be part of the family pictures at my son's wedding!"

We all were shocked. Why in the world would our friend be so stubborn about having her picture taken? After much coaxing, Betty finally shared why she felt so strongly.

"I know how ugly I am," she said softly. "I've learned to accept the way I look, but seeing pictures just reminds me of it all over again."

I wanted to cry! It broke my heart that such a precious woman could have such a warped perception of herself. Betty was no beauty queen, but neither were any of the rest of us. Whatever she lacked in physical attractiveness, she more than made up for in the kind, gentle spirit that attracted all of us. We all could see the undeniable beauty radiating from within her. Why couldn't *she?*

God designed each of us to depend on him. Without doing so, we can never live up to our fullest potential.

My friend Betty's story is a powerful example of how the enemy relishes messing with our heads and our hearts. It doesn't matter to him whether your self-image is overinflated or underinflated. Either type of distortion is just as effective for cluttering your life and keeping you away from the truth. Satan knows that if you overrate your value and your ability to take care of yourself, you will see no need for a close relationship with God. Why bother when you can do it all yourself? The end result is a self-centered and self-gratifying life. On the other hand, if you undervalue yourself, you will tend to shy away from intimacy with God. You will keep God at arm's length because you don't feel worthy of his time and attention. The result is a life without the healing power of God's love.

Either way, our adversary wins and you lose—big time.

How God Sees Us

Scripture tells us again and again how very precious we are to God. He doesn't just *like* us. He is so enthralled with each of us that even the very hairs of our heads are all numbered (Matthew 10:30).

Ephesians 2:10 tells us, "We are God's workmanship, created in Christ Jesus to do good works, which God prepared in advance for us to do." We are God's works of art. Like a master sculptor, he took great pains in tenderly crafting each of us. But this verse also tells us we are his instruments, to be used by him as he sees fit. We were not created for our own pleasure but for God's pleasure and his purposes. He never intended for us to go it alone but to cooperate with him in his master plan. God designed each of us to depend on him. Without doing so, we can never live up to our fullest potential.

Leonie is my prayer partner in Australia. Leonie has a powerful testimony of how she learned that she is not as self-sufficient as she once thought.

"I always considered myself the very definition of *sanity*," Leonie shared with me. "Yes, I'd had my ups and downs, but I always bounced back. And I had very little sympathy for those I knew who suffered from clinical depression."

Then, only a couple of years ago, Leonie experienced her own bout with clinical depression. The depression became so debilitating that she needed to be treated in a psychiatric hospital. There she was faced with electric shock therapy if she wasn't able to start eating again. It was, ultimately, an eye-opening time for her.

Understanding our place in God's plan clarifies our lives because it gives us a clearer picture of who we are and what our lives should be about.

"Over that week, I made up my mind that I needed to rely on God far more and me far less," she said. "No matter how many abilities I had, no matter how brilliant I thought myself, I realized I could not survive without God's help."

Think about the second part of the Clarity Principle: "Let us run with perseverance the race marked out for us." Having a proper view of ourselves helps us run the way we were made to run. God never intended for us to run completely on our own, willy-nilly as our whims direct. Likewise, he never planned for us to run in a cowering position as if we're not worthy to be in the race. Ironically, God wired us in such a way that as we seek to bring him pleasure, he gives us pleasure in the form of purpose and meaning in our lives. Understanding our place in God's plan clarifies our lives because it gives us a clearer picture of who we are and what our lives should be about.

Seeing ourselves as God sees us also encompasses the third part of the Clarity Principle: "Let us fix our eyes on Jesus." If we ever wonder how valuable we are to God, we need only to remember what Jesus endured on the cross. Jesus' crucifixion was not Satan's triumph but rather God's perfectly designed plan. What kind of father would willingly put his own son through such torture and shame? Only a Father who loves the rest of his children as much as God loves us.

UNDOING the DISTORTION

Made by the almighty God for his almighty purposes—the very thought of it is both humbling and exhilarating at the same time! I am humbled to know that I am utterly dependent on God. But I am also exhilarated when I think of the possibilities of an infinite God working through me.

I haven't always been able to see myself as God does. I remember the wonder and doubt I felt as a teen when a friend first helped me to understand the profound truth expressed in the children's song "Jesus Loves Me." Pam was a new Christian. In her excitement about her newfound faith, she had no problem believing she was valuable to God. I, on the other hand, had gone to church all my life but never fully embraced this reality.

"Nancy, God loves you," Pam said. "Jesus loves you. He's crazy about you." Her zeal was contagious, and for first time I began to feel in my heart that it was true.

I am humbled to know that I am utterly dependent on God. But I am also exhilarated when I think of the possibilities of an infinite God working through me.

How about you? Do you have a God-inspired view of yourself? Or do you vacillate between acting as if you don't need him and then wondering why he would help you if you *did* ask for his help? Here are three strategies for moving from a distorted view of yourself to one that is more in line with God's view:

READ THE BIBLE TO SEE WHAT GOD SAYS. Dive into God's Word to discover what it teaches about our relationship with our creator. The Bible is where God's personality and character are revealed. The psalms are filled with glimpses of God's great love and care for us: "The LORD takes delight in his people" (Psalm 149:4); "What is man that you are mindful of him? . . . You made him a little lower than heavenly beings and crowned him with glory and honor" (Psalm 8:4, 5); "I praise you because I am fearfully and wonderfully made" (Psalm 139:14). The psalms also remind us of our undeniable need for God: "You are my Lord; apart from you I have no good thing" (Psalm 16:2); "He lifted me out of the slimy pit. . . . He set my feet on a rock and gave me a firm place to stand" (Psalm 40:2). Meditate on Scriptures that give you a clearer picture of yourself from God's perspective.

ASK GOD TO REVEAL YOUR MISCONCEPTIONS. While you're digging deep into the way God sees things, ask him to show you any areas in which your view of yourself is inaccurate. Is your self-image bulging like an overstuffed handbag, or is it droopy and squishy like an old helium balloon? Even if your assessment of yourself is usually fairly accurate, ask him to reveal situations in which you are tempted to veer to one extreme or the other.

DEVELOP A GOD'S-EYE VIEW. God wants you to be neither overconfident nor underconfident. He wants you to revel in both your worth to him and your need for him. Ask him to give you the kind of self-confidence he wants you to have. Request also that he remove anything in your life that stands in the way of this.

Has your self-image been distorted in one way or another? Are these faulty perceptions holding you back from cooperating with God in his master plan? If so, it's time to get rid of this clutter for good. Say good-bye to the confusion of defective self-perceptions so you can welcome the clarity of God's perspective with open arms.

CLUTTER *BUSTERS*

◆ Are you comfortable with the idea of being totally dependent on God? Is dependence on God easier to imagine in some areas of your life than in others?

◆ What keeps you from seeing yourself as God sees you?

◆ Have you ever experienced a major crisis, as Leonie did, that forced you to acknowledge your need for God's intervention in your life? In what ways does that experience impact how you live today?

COMING INTO CLARITY

As a child, I never quite felt that I measured up to my parents' expectations. This resulted in a low self-esteem that followed me into adulthood. This negative view of myself continued until one day God reminded me that what Jesus called the second commandment doesn't stop with "Love your neighbor"; it says to love my neighbor as myself.

The Lord impressed on my heart that as things were, my neighbor couldn't possibly receive much love because I had so little love for myself. To truly obey this commandment, I had to learn to love myself. Since that time, he has brought people and events into my life to show me that he indeed does have my picture on his refrigerator! God's continual and often miraculous provisions are an exclamation point to his love for me as he has met all my needs.

Susan
Charlotte, North Carolina

from cluttered lifestyle to outer clarity

Be very careful, then, how you live—not as unwise but as wise, making the most of every opportunity.

EPHESIANS 5:15, 16

Do not store up for yourselves treasures on earth, where moth and rust destroy, and where thieves break in and steal. But store up for yourselves treasures in heaven. . . . For where your treasure is, there your heart will be also.

MATTHEW 6:19-21

EIGHT

GOOD-BYE, CLUTTER!
I'm done with commitment overload! I'm ready to start using the word **no** *as a powerful tool to help me manage my time.*

---

no is
not a dirty
word

When someone asks you how you are, what do you usually say? If you're like most women, your automatic response is probably "Fine." I used to give that same standard response too—until my friend Margaret shared something that changed my perspective.

"Nancy, people today always say 'Fine' when you ask them how they are," Margaret mused. "But that's not what they mean at all."

Hmm, I thought. *Where is she going with this?*

"When people say 'Fine,'" Margaret continued, "what they really mean is that they are Frustrated, Irritated, Neurotic, and Exhausted."

Isn't that true? Look around at the women you know. We may not be neurotic, but many of us are running on fumes. Every day, we are stretched taut like a rubber band waiting to snap. Demands from our spouses, children, employers, friends, neighbors, and church—there never seems to be enough of ourselves to go around. In trying to please everyone, we end up depleted and depressed, overtaxed and overwhelmed.

There are enough good things out there to keep us busy 24/7. But saying yes to all of them means we say no to other things that are truly more important.

Is your schedule so full that you hardly have time to breathe, much less help out with causes near and dear to your heart? Do you often feel torn between what you want to do and what you feel others expect of you? Do the appointments on your calendar reflect your priorities, or do they reflect your inability to say no?

For busy career women, wives, and mothers, wasting time is usually not our problem. We face another kind of challenge: sorting through all we could be doing to find what we *should* be doing. There are enough good things out there to keep us busy 24/7. But saying yes to all of them means we say no to other things that are truly more important. Being yes-women means that the values we want to make our priority—marriage, children, friendships, our walk with God—are often neglected while we devote much more time and energy to less consequential things. Clarifying means learning to look past the endless demands for our attention in order to align our schedules with our values.

Do you ever feel guilty for not being able to juggle all the plates in your life without dropping a few? If so, that's exactly how Satan wants you to feel. He loves to seduce you into saying yes to too many things and then make you feel guilty for not doing them all well. He knows that you, as a woman, are likely to have difficulty setting boundaries. He also knows that many women take pride and pleasure in being the one who cares for everyone else. If he can clutter your life by keeping you focused on the trivial many, you won't have time for the vital few, and you'll have no energy at all to respond to the call of God.

Martha's Mistake

If ever there was a woman who lost control of her priorities, it was Martha, whose story is recorded in Luke 10. Poor Martha. Too bad she will forever be remembered as the one who was more concerned about making dinner than making Jesus feel welcome in her home!

Clarifying means learning to look past the endless demands for our attention in order to align our schedules with our values.

What separates Martha from her sister Mary is that Martha did not order her time by her priorities. She may have sincerely thought that welcoming Jesus was most important, but her behavior did not reflect that. It's as if she had a choice of visiting with Jesus or vacuuming, and she chose the vacuum. It's not that Mary didn't help out with the chores. I believe she did—perhaps she helped cook and did the dishes before Jesus arrived. But once Jesus set foot in their home, Mary dropped the busywork in favor of what really mattered—spending quality time with her Lord.

Jesus' response to Martha is just as applicable to us as it was to her: "Martha, Martha! You are worried and upset about so many things, but only one thing is necessary. Mary has chosen what is best, and it will not be taken away from her" (Luke 10:41, 42, *CEV*). Be honest now. Don't we all make Martha's mistake? We mean well. We want to help out in our children's school and be active in our communities and do our part at church. As with Martha's cooking and cleaning, there's nothing inherently wrong with any of these activities. The problem is when they become a hindrance and keep us from doing what really matters—spending quality time with our Lord and the people he puts in our paths.

Michelle is a modern-day Mary. Michelle has a home-based child care business. Years ago, when she first considered starting her business, she dismissed the idea because she had always struggled with keeping the clutter in her home under control. How could she open her messy home to other families? What would the parents think if her home wasn't always clean and neat?

Learning to live our priorities actually encompasses all three parts of the Clarity Principle.

Michelle finally decided it was more important to offer personalized, quality care for children who needed it rather than to worry about keeping a spotless house. Although she sometimes felt self-conscious about the 1988 station wagon in her driveway, the threadbare couch in her den, and the daily mess she struggled to control around her house, she didn't let that distract her from her top priority: providing the best possible care for the children in her charge.

"Just this morning one of my clients was telling me about her experiences with another child care provider who cares for her daughter on a different day," Michelle told me. "I've seen that provider's house, and it is beautiful with expensive furniture way too special for the children to sit on. All she has is one carefully chosen box of toys."

Life is much simpler when your values and decisions are clear and your decisions clearly support your values.

Michelle's client complained that her daughter doesn't like the other provider's house as much as Michelle's. When Michelle commented, "It's such a beautiful house though," her client replied, "Yes, but your house is a *home.*"

Michelle's story is a good example of what it means to put first things first. Learning to live our priorities actually encompasses all three parts of the Clarity Principle. Getting rid of extraneous obligations and expectations is one of the ways we "throw off everything that hinders." Not letting the trivial supersede the vital is an example of how we "run with perseverance the race marked out for us." And ordering our lives around what God wants is part of how we "fix our eyes on Jesus."

When you truly put first things first, all other things fall in line. Confusion dissipates. Decisions are much less difficult. If an activity or commitment fits with what you value most and what you believe God is calling you to do, the answer is yes. If an activity or commitment *doesn't* fit with your priorities, the answer is an unapologetic no. Instead of feeling torn, you can rest in the knowledge that you are right on target—putting your energy where it needs to be.

Life is much simpler when your values and decisions are clear and your decisions clearly support your values.

WHEN to SAY YES, WHEN to SAY NO

I admit I sometimes hear voices. Not audible voices but, rather, that clear, inner voice I've come to recognize as God's way of sometimes telling me things he wants me to know.

Saying no is one of the biggest challenges we face.

During the time that Lydia attended our church's child care program, our family became fond of the preschool's director, Mrs. Mary. Never have I met anyone with such a heart for children. Because we thought so highly of Mrs. Mary, imagine what my first thoughts were one day when she told me the child care program was in desperate need of help. A couple of teachers had just left the program, and Mrs. Mary was looking for new employees to fill the vacancies. But in the interim, parents were asked to do what they could to help out.

Maybe I could spare a morning or two a week, I thought. At the time I was in a busy season of writing. I was also heading up a prayer group and helping out with a Sunday school class at church. I had more than a full plate.

I could rearrange my schedule, I speculated, *and get up a little earlier each day.* I was already rising at 4:00 AM to get in a few hours of work before Lydia woke up. How much earlier did I think I could get up?

Then I heard it. The words were so clear and concise, I knew better than to question what I heard: "Tend your own garden!"

Wanting to support Mrs. Mary was honorable. Helping fill the vacancies was a good thing, but not one of the best things God was calling me to do. When I thought about it that way, how could I say anything but no to that part of me that wanted to say "Sure, I'll help"?

For many of us, saying no is one of the biggest challenges we face. How do we learn to stop trying to do everything so we can do well the few things God has called us to do? Here are some strategies that have worked for me:

BE CLEAR ABOUT YOUR PRIORITIES. This may sound like a no-brainer. Of course, your first priorities are God, your spouse, and your children. But be more specific. In your mind, what does it mean to put God first? What does it mean to be a good wife and mom? Does being a good mother have to include being soccer mom and den mother every year? Does being a committed Christian mean you must be involved with every project your church sponsors?

CLASSIFY YOUR PRIORITIES IN ORDER OF IMPORTANCE. As you identify your priorities, it is also helpful to make your own good-better-best list of the various commitments in your life. Even within the scope of things that support your core values, inevitably there will be some things that are more beneficial and more supportive of your values than others. For example, having your kids in one extracurricular activity per year may support the priority you place on raising well-rounded children. Allowing more than one sport or club per year may fall into the "good" category—something you'd do only if it didn't endanger carrying out any of the things in the "best" category.

SET A TIME BUDGET FOR ADDITIONAL COMMITMENTS. Once you're sure what you should focus on, set a limit for how much time you can devote to things that are good but not the best use of your time and energy. How many hours per week can you spare without cutting into the time needed to tend to your own priorities? After looking at your list of most important obligations, you may realize that you can allot only two additional hours per week to good-but-not-best commitments. Use this limit as your guide in accepting or declining additional commitments. When considering something new, remember that in order to stay within your time budget, you must take away one previous commitment for every new one you add.

<u>No</u> is not a dirty word. Let go of being a yes-woman so you can be a woman who truly knows how to put first things first.

Are you tired of living in conflict over trying to do it all? Do you want to learn to say no without guilt and yes without sacrificing your sanity? If so, it's time to move from clutter to clarity. *No* is not a dirty word. Let go of being a yes-woman so you can be a woman who truly knows how to put first things first.

CLUTTER *BUSTERS*

◆ When has your saying yes to good things meant saying no to other things that were truly more important?

◆ Are you more like Martha or Mary? Are there times when, despite your good intentions, your behavior is not consistent with what you say you value most? What causes you to act in ways that don't line up with your values?

◆ Think about this statement: "Tend your own garden!" What do you consider to be your garden—the best things God has assigned you to put in the place of priority above all other good things?

COMING INTO CLARITY

When my child was young, my family was extremely active in our church. My biggest jobs were coordinating the church nursery and directing the senior choir. I was stretched to the max, and I began getting up at 3:00 AM to get work done before my child was awake.

At first, I thought this was a great idea, but little did I know I was heading down a path of self-destruction. Fortunately, after a few brief illnesses and extreme fatigue, I figured out I was no good to anyone if I wasn't healthy. That meant I had to take some things off my proverbial plate.

When I resigned as choir director, I received letters from some very upset choir members and others for being "selfish." I could have let the church members' letters defeat me or bully me into taking the position back, but I held firm. Satan was pulling me into a huge guilt trip, but I learned that I can survive all the cruel things people say when they are looking from the outside in. I learned to make decisions based on what is best, not on what will keep the largest number of other people happy.

Kelly
Frederick, Maryland

NINE

GOOD-BYE, CLUTTER!
No more soul snacks for me. I'm ready to build time into my day for real spiritual nutrition, and I and won't be satisfied with anything less.

---

too busy
for God

Michael and I enjoy traveling, and we try to stay in hotels that offer a free continental breakfast. The spread usually consists of a variety of pastries, cereal, fresh fruit, yogurt, juice, and coffee. If we're lucky, we may also have the choice of hot foods such as scrambled eggs, waffles, or biscuits and gravy.

That's what continental breakfast usually means, but not always. The definition depends on the establishment. You never know exactly what you'll find. Michael and I have been disappointed many times when what we expected to find was not at all what was offered. This has happened so frequently that now when we check in to a hotel we've never visited before, we often engage in a little lighthearted speculation about what we'll find when we go downstairs for breakfast the next morning. "So what will it be? Day-old doughnuts or soggy sausage and biscuits?"

It's not that we don't appreciate the convenience of having breakfast—however skimpy it may be—offered by the hotel. The problem is that we are usually hungry again in just a few hours. These quick breakfasts may be tasty at the moment, but the high-carb—and typically high-sugar—foods don't satisfy for very long. We usually have to stop for something else a couple of hours down the road.

I've noticed the same thing goes for my spiritual life. It takes more than a small serving of prayer or a snack-pack of inspirational reading to satisfy my spiritual appetite. I can try to get by on quick spiritual snacks, but my heart and spirit soon feel empty again, because I didn't give them the full meal they needed.

On a scale of one to ten, how's your spiritual hunger level? Do you often find your spirit rumbling because your last spiritual nibble didn't fill the bill? When life is hectic, do you try to get by on quick and easy spiritual snacks when what you truly need are real meals? Does your relationship with God feel less like a hearty breakfast and more like a quick cup of coffee to go?

I can try to get by on quick spiritual snacks, but my heart and spirit soon feel empty again.

By outward appearances we all seem to be well fed. But what if we could see inside? What if we had a spiritual X-ray machine that showed whether our spirits were adequately nourished or on the brink of starvation?

SPIRITUAL SNACKING

Unfortunately for many of us, spiritual snacking is the norm rather than the exception. We want to connect with God, but our schedules are so full that a quick prayer or an occasional glance at the Scriptures is all we can manage. We know we need a balanced diet for our spirits, yet we just can't seem to find time to make it happen.

Is it possible to be too busy for God? Our adversary loves to make us think so. Keeping us too occupied to connect with God is one of his favorite tricks. It doesn't matter to him what we busy ourselves with, but being the sly dog that he is, he particularly enjoys using things we think we're doing for God to keep us from spending quality time with God. As we talked about in the previous chapter, we can easily become so caught up in doing good things that seem important that we can't find time to do the things that are vital. And the most necessary of those is staying in close contact with God.

> *Is it possible to be too busy for God?*
> *Our adversary loves to make us think so.*

Satan knows we won't last long without adequate spiritual nourishment and that in our modern-day mind-set, quiet time seems like wasted time. That's why he continues to feed us the line that we don't have time to spend with God. The truth is that spending time with God is the most important thing we'll do all day! Our spiritual health depends on it.

Failing to make time for God complicates life by keeping us focused on our own abilities—what we can accomplish within any given day. We're afraid that if we slow down, we'll lose ground, but actually the opposite is true: by taking time to fuel up, we plug in to God. He has infinite ability to work wonders with our time, and when we give him the first portion of it, we put ourselves in a position to gain ground.

THE IMPACT of QUIET MOMENTS

"Don't just stand there. Do something!" How many times have you heard that, or said it? In our warp-speed world, we think that unless we are moving forward at a furious pace, we are not accomplishing anything of value. That is one of the reasons why it is so hard for many of us to spend time alone with God. Somehow it doesn't feel right to be sitting still, reading the Bible, praying, or journaling quietly, when there's so much around us to be done. But what we don't realize is that those quiet moments of "doing nothing" have a great impact on the rest of the day.

Just ask Rena. She has her own story to tell about the importance of taking time to connect with God. "I just recently realized that I can't function properly without my private time with God," Rena told me.

What does God want you to do when the demands of life press in? Listen again to what Psalm 46:10 says.

Normally Rena wakes up early every day to pray, for the needs of her church as well as for herself and her own needs. But one week she felt particularly tired and didn't get up for her prayer time several days in a row.

On one of those days, Rena had some errands to run but didn't feel up to getting out. She sensed something wrong, so she asked for God's guidance as to whether she should leave the house that day or not. Usually she can sense God's leading, but that day was different. Normally, the lack of clear direction would have been a red flag for Rena, but because she had a lot to do, she decided to go out anyway. Big mistake!

"The stores had none of the items I needed," Rena remembers. "Then I ran the car over something and had a flat tire on the way home. It wasn't just an ordinary flat either. The tire was shredded all the way down to the rim before I could get to a tire center."

Rena is convinced that she could have avoided a lot of hassle and heartache that day if only she had taken time to connect with God.

Being still doesn't come naturally for most of us, but did you know that the Bible actually commands it? Psalm 46:10 says, "Be still, and know that I am God." And Psalm 37:7 tells us, "Be still before the LORD and wait patiently for him." He is the one over everything. Nothing is beyond his abilities; nothing is headed your way that he doesn't already know about. No matter what pressing needs or urgent demands are on your schedule, he wants to be included—not excluded because you think you cannot squeeze him in.

What does God want you to do when the demands of life press in? Listen again to what Psalm 46:10 says. Got a big assignment due at work? *Be still, and know that I am God.* Are there children who constantly need your attention? Is housework piling up all around you? *Be still, and know that I am God.* Is your family in a financial hole or, worse, a financial crisis? *Be still, and know that I am God.* Whatever is going on in your life, he wants you to rest in the confidence that he is in control.

Remember the second part of the Clarity Principle: "Let us run with perseverance the race marked out for us." How can we run the race on an empty tank? We can't because we don't have the resources we need. In our own strength we can't deal with everything life throws our way. Connecting with God regularly clarifies life because it fills our tanks with the spiritual fuel we need.

MAKING IT HAPPEN

Lydia loves having a clean room. But does that mean her room always stays that way? Not by a long shot! Hardly a day goes by without drawers left open, dirty clothes strewn across the room, toys littering the floor. Lydia lacks the self-discipline to actually make a clean room happen on a regular basis.

The habit of regularly feeding my spirit began in that little apartment in Japan and has stuck with me ever since.

When it comes to having regular time alone with God, many of us are like Lydia and her room. The problem is not that we don't see the need for God's presence in our lives; we simply aren't disciplined enough to make it happen on a regular basis.

Maybe that is the challenge you face. Try as you might, you just can't put yourself on a regular "spiritual feeding schedule." For years I was in a similar situation. With all the demands of work and school, I hardly had time to feed my stomach, much less my spirit. Consequently, my spiritual life was in shambles. And without proper spiritual nutrition, I didn't have the strength to deal with challenges and temptations.

The turning point came when I graduated from college and went to Japan to teach English for a year. For the first time in my life, I found myself desperately dependent on God. In an unfamiliar country where I couldn't speak the language, stomach the food, or call home anytime I wanted, I needed God's help every day. I learned quickly that if I wanted to stay connected to God, effort on my part was required.

I started by getting up early. I was used to waking early to study for college classes, so I just switched the emphasis of my study from academics to spiritual matters. Those regular times of prayer and Bible reading over a hot cup of tea recharged my spiritual batteries and gave me strength to face the challenges of living thousands of miles from home. The habit of regularly feeding my spirit began in that little apartment in Japan and has stuck with me ever since. Looking back, I see that it wasn't until I made time with God a priority that I actually began to mature as a Christian.

How does someone go from occasional snacking to a balanced spiritual diet? Consider these steps to help you move in that direction:

COMMIT TO CHANGE. You have to make a decision to do something different than whatever you've been doing. If you've never before tried to make quiet time with God a habit, commit to yourself and to God to start building that habit. If your attempts at a regular rendezvous with God have been sketchy, make a pledge to become more disciplined in this area.

FIND YOUR BEST TIME. Part of making a commitment is finding a time you are most likely to be able to commit to with regularity. If the thought of getting up early sends chills down your spine, what other regularly occurring times might work for you? Your lunch hour at work? Your children's afternoon nap? In the evenings after the kids go to bed? Whatever time you choose, make it a standing appointment, the same as any other appointment on your calendar. Write it in your planner or on your to-do list.

BE INVENTIVE. If your schedule is hectic, you may have to be creative about the time you can claim as yours and God's. Even small chunks of time can make a big difference if you are intentional about how you use them. One busy mother I know uses her baby's midnight feedings as her prayer time. She's up anyway; why not use that time to talk to God? Another woman I know leaves for work fifteen minutes early each day and stops by a nearby park for Scripture reading and meditation. Think creatively as you look for ways to capture opportunities that would otherwise be lost.

SET YOURSELF UP FOR SUCCESS. Start with small, attainable goals—ten minutes of prayer each morning or fifteen minutes of devotional reading each night—and work your way up. Be flexible too. If one method doesn't work well, try something else until you find what works for you. And if you don't initially feel that you are connecting with God, don't get discouraged! In my experience, spiritual growth is 20 percent feeling and 80 percent doing. Keep reaching out for God and putting yourself in a place to connect with him.

Think creatively as you look for ways to capture opportunities that would otherwise be lost.

Have you had enough of spiritual snacks? Are you ready to move on to satisfying meals? Don't let a busy schedule keep you from getting proper spiritual nutrition. Experience the clarity of being still and plugging in to God so you can be rid of spiritual starvation once and for all.

CLUTTER *BUSTERS*

◆ What symptoms do you experience when your spirit is hungry for time alone with God?

◆ Have you had experiences similar to Rena's that helped you see the importance of connecting with God before tackling all your other obligations?

◆ If you struggle with finding a daily, consistent time for quiet time, what pockets of time throughout your week could you use creatively for this purpose?

COMING INTO CLARITY

In my years of being a Christian, I've learned something about making time for God. I believe we are supposed to find God in all things. Although quiet time with God is essential, I now feel it is equally essential to see God in the midst of our busyness.

Am I busy with meetings today? Then there is probably someone in one of those meetings whom God is calling me to meet—someone who needs to be acknowledged or needs to see my example of being fed by God. Are there errands I need to run? As I buy groceries, pay bills, pick up clothes from the cleaners, I take that opportunity to thank God for my abundance. I don't wait until my quiet time. I do it minute after minute throughout my day. Our digestive system works to deliver nourishment to our bodies between our meals. Likewise, I have found that acknowledging God keeps me sustained between my conversations with him.

Adela
Aurora, Colorado

TEN

GOOD-BYE, CLUTTER!
*I'm tired of living in a state of excess. I've let my life be
complicated long enough by too many possessions.*

---

making peace with our possessions

A sk a group of average American women whether they have
too many clothes, and most of them will probably look at
you as if you've lost your mind. *What? Too many clothes? Does such
a possibility even exist?* But not everyone in the world feels that
way. Certainly not my friend Yulia, who was born and raised
in Belarus. She and her husband, Craig, spend the majority of
their time there, but usually come to visit Craig's family in the
States every year or so for several months at a time.

During their visits, Yulia often receives many hand-me-
downs from American friends. She also has fun shopping
for bargains at yard sales and thrift stores. Although she
enjoys having so many nice things to wear during her visits,
this influx creates a problem Yulia never encounters in her
home country.

"I don't need many clothes in Belarus," Yulia says. "I can
wear the same outfit two or three days in a row, and that's fine
with me." At home, her wardrobe is simple but

more than enough to meet her needs. In America, she is faced with more choices than she knows what to do with. "When we're here, I have to spend time thinking about what I want to wear each day," she explains. "With so many outfits to choose from, I worry about making sure I wear them all."

Instead of being served by what we own, we end up serving our possessions with inordinate amounts of our time and energy.

Isn't it curious how quickly roles can be reversed? Possessions that are supposed to enrich our lives often drain us instead. Things we think will make our lives better only bring additional heartache and hassle. Instead of being served by what we own, we end up serving our possessions with inordinate amounts of our time and energy. Like Yulia, we may soon realize that owning more can actually be a burden rather than a blessing.

POSSESSED BY OUR POSSESSIONS

Unneeded possessions are clutter—clutter that robs us of space, time, and peace of mind.

Do you ever feel crowded out of your own home by all your family's belongings? Does having everything you need seem to have turned into having more than you can ever use? Are you overwhelmed by the effort and expense required to clean, maintain, insure, and store all the stuff that is supposed to make life simpler? If you give material possessions an inch, they will quickly become your ruler, your measure of the quality and success of your life. At that point, you are possessed by your possessions.

Clutter, as we noted in chapter 1, is anything that has outlived its usefulness in your life. Think of clutter as a risky venture. Despite all the effort you invest in your things—and how much aggravation that causes—you get very little in return. Notice those last few words. Whether something is clutter depends on what you get out of it.

Because clutter is too much of things that contribute too little, it disrupts the equilibrium in your life.

Women sometimes fall into the clutter trap simply because we can't cut the emotional ties we have with our things. Sometimes we use clutter to insulate ourselves and give ourselves a sense of security. We think that if we surround ourselves with enough things—a year's supply of toilet paper or shoes for every possible clothing combination, for example—then somehow we will feel safe. Those who are frugal by nature find that even frugality can contribute to clutter: in our efforts to be thrifty, we cross over the line from saving to hoarding.

Despite all the effort you invest in your things,
you get very little in return.

Too much of anything creates imbalance and instability. And Satan loves it when you are off balance, because then you are vulnerable. As long as you are distracted, you can't focus on what's most important. As long as you are emotionally tied to your things, Satan has you right where he wants you—looking to anything and everything but God to fill your needs.

WHEN to HOLD ON, WHEN to LET GO

Dealing with clutter means knowing when to let go of things that no longer meet our needs. The writer of Ecclesiastes puts it this way: "There is a time for everything, and a season for every activity under heaven . . . a time to keep and a time to throw away" (Ecclesiastes 3:1, 6).

Clutter quickly multiplies when we don't temper our saving and acquiring with a healthy dose of discarding and giving away. But knowing when to hold on and when to let go clarifies our lives by restoring equilibrium and preventing our possessions from taking over.

A few years ago I received letters from two different women who had recently gone through intense seasons of throwing away. The first woman, who identified herself only as A.K., said she was motivated to pare down her belongings after realizing just how little all her things really meant to her. Although A.K. is happy now to be free of so much clutter around her house, she still cringes when she thinks about how much money she spent on all those things she ended up giving away.

Clutter quickly multiplies when we don't temper our saving and acquiring with a healthy dose of discarding and giving away.

The other woman who wrote had a different motivation for tackling clutter. Angie and her husband were planning to move from a large home with ample storage to a much smaller apartment. Because Angie is by nature a pack rat, the process of purging had been painful for her, but she could see it had been a growth experience. She considered it to be a lesson from God about what she should and should not treasure in her life.

Does God care about your clutter? The answer to that question is found in the first part of the Clarity Principle: "Let us throw off everything that hinders." If the clutter weighs you down and keeps you from developing the potential God has placed in you, then the answer is yes. He wants you to live in balance. He wants you to get your sense of security from him, not from a closet packed with clothes or a cabinet overflowing with gadgets.

God wants you to have a right relationship with your possessions so that *you* control *them,* not the other way around.

RAISING a BABY in a GARBAGE HEAP

In our home, Michael and I have a motto we live by: Space promotes peace. This slogan is not something that we came up with. It's something we learned from Rhonda, a friend who is a professional organizer and teaches classes on getting organized and managing clutter. Rhonda is an excellent teacher because she can truly empathize with those who struggle with clutter. She has an interesting story of what put her on the road to permanent clutter control.

Although she was raised by a super-organized mom, Rhonda, for the first two years of her marriage, used none of the skills her mother had taught her for keeping a home in order. Her home life was ruled by chaos and clutter.

"The turning point for me came one day when I was dressing my baby daughter up in several new outfits I'd bought," Rhonda says. "I had decided to take pictures for the grandparents. I had to literally clear piles off the table to make space for my daughter's carrier."

When Rhonda got the pictures back from the photo lab, they showed a beautiful baby surrounded by piles of junk.

"It was then that I realized what I was doing. God had given me this beautiful little flower, and I was raising her in a garbage heap," Rhonda says. "I knew right then and there that something had to change." Slowly but surely, Rhonda did change her behavior and her attitude toward clutter. Now she uses her experiences to help other people see that they can too.

How to Make Peace with Your Possessions

So how does a person make the kind of changes Rhonda did? These guidelines will help:

BE HONEST WITH YOURSELF ABOUT THE EXTENT TO WHICH CLUTTER RULES YOUR LIFE. Do you often hold onto things you don't really need, or don't even care for, simply because you can't part with them? In an effort to stock up, have you given up valuable space in your home? The yardstick for measuring clutter is how much value something gives back in relation to the time, space, and effort it requires. Take a good look around your home and see how your things measure up to this test.

DETERMINE WHAT SHOULD GO. As you begin deciding what to keep and what to toss or give away, ask yourself these questions: How long has it been since I used this item? If I haven't used it in several months or years, is it because the item never really fit or worked right in the first place? Do I already own something else that can serve the same purpose as this item? Can I get from some other source the information this item contains, such as from the library or on the Internet?

PLAN YOUR WORK AND WORK YOUR PLAN. One very practical decluttering tactic is to have three boxes or bags handy while working: one for things to throw away, one for things to give away, and one for things to sell. When decluttering, it is easy to become distracted if you don't know exactly what to do with something. Having these specific containers makes the task easier because your choices are laid out right there in front of you. And when you're done working for the day, cleanup is easy too. Simply empty the "throw away" box into the garbage can and put the "give away" box in your car to drop off at a local charity the next time you're out. Store items from your "sell" box in a closet, the attic, or the garage until your next yard sale.

The yardstick for measuring clutter is how much value something gives back in relation to the time, space, and effort it requires.

Even with this system, the thought of dealing with all your clutter at one time may be overwhelming. You may feel you have so much to do that you don't even know where to start. If so, attack the task of decluttering in little chunks. Set a timer, and work at clutter control for thirty minutes at a time. If thirty minutes is too much for you, try ten or fifteen.

Another way to make the task easier is to focus on one cluttered room or area at a time. You can break down that particular area into bite-size tasks too: one side of the closet first, then the other, then the desk, and then the chest of drawers. Keep working at it a little at a time until the clutter in that area is gone.

DON'T TRY TO DO THIS ALONE. As with any major undertaking, increase your chances for success by bathing your task in prayer. Ask God to help you learn to let go when letting go is appropriate. If fear is at the root of your hoarding things away, ask him to reveal this to you and show you ways to replace that fear with confidence in his provision. If unhealthy emotions keep you tied to things, request that God give you strength to confront the past and settle any unfinished business so you can move on.

DO REGULAR DECLUTTERING MAINTENANCE. Keep clutter under control by doing short maintenance sessions on a routine basis. It's much easier to carve out ten minutes every few days to organize a small mess than to find an hour or two to organize a large mess resulting from weeks of neglect. Just as regular exercise is necessary to maintain good physical fitness, regular sorting and purging is necessary to maintain a clutter-free home.

Keep clutter under control by doing short maintenance sessions on a routine basis.

Have you had enough of living as a slave to clutter? Are you determined not to live that way any longer? Now is the time to clarify and put clutter in its place—out of your life for good. Give clutter a farewell kiss so you can take back control of your home and your life.

CLUTTER *BUSTERS*

◆ When have you felt controlled by your possessions? What did you do—or what do you need to do—to take back control?

◆ What are some evidences that having more than you need actually creates imbalance and instability in your life?

◆ Think about Rhonda's story of seeing her daughter as a precious flower growing in a garbage heap. Are there any "flowers" that are struggling to grow amid all the unneeded possessions in your home?

COMING INTO CLARITY

I am turning the big 5-0 soon, and I recently realized I am tired of spending my life taking care of things. I sat down and evaluated my life and what is really important to me. Do you know what? It isn't stuff! The more I own, the more time I have to spend dusting, cleaning, straightening up, and spending money on it.

It is absolutely liberating not to have my life controlled by the material things surrounding me. In the past there have been times when I wanted to go somewhere or just sit down and read a book, but I had this nagging feeling that I should be doing something else—like managing the things in my home. Not having so much to care for frees up my time to spend making memories with my family and friends. Spiritually, I am more inclined to listen to God's whisper to get involved in his work when I don't have so many possessions shouting that they need my time and attention.

My family has a history of longevity, so I'm anticipating living another fifty years. I want to start this next phase of my life with only the things that make me happy and don't require constant upkeep on my part.

Candy
Cordova, Tennessee

ELEVEN

GOOD-BYE, CLUTTER!

I can get along just fine without all the techno-craze. From now on, if a piece of technology doesn't clarify my life, it's outta here!

---

escaping
the technology
trap

I'll admit—on a scale of one to ten, I'm about a six when it comes to being technologically savvy. My family's livelihood depends on the Internet, so I am very comfortable using e-mail and the Web, and I have a cell phone. But that's about it.

I enjoy using my cell phone when I need to, although most days it stays in my purse without even being turned on. When I got the phone, I bought a pay-as-you-go model for two reasons: I didn't want a monthly payment, and I wanted an incentive to use it only when truly necessary.

But what is considered necessary use of a cell phone? The definition varies widely. For some of us, necessary use means talking to anyone and everyone about anything and everything all the time. Once when I was in a public restroom, I heard a woman in one of the stalls conducting the normal business one conducts in a restroom stall *while* she talked casually and comfortably on her cell phone, as if she were sitting on her couch at home. She never missed a beat!

I was stunned. *Is nothing sacred?* I thought. At that moment I made a decision: unless I need to call 911, I will never conduct phone calls while using the toilet!

How connected do we really need to be?

TRAPPED BY GADGETS and GIZMOS

Are you surrounded by electronic devices—cell phones, computers, PDAs, pagers, iPods, and MP3 players—constantly competing for your attention? Has the technology that was supposed to help organize your life actually begun to take over your life? Do you find that the more time you spend writing e-mail and leaving voice-mail messages, the less in touch you are with those around you?

Just as Adam and Eve's knowledge of good and evil came at a price, technological advances have their price too.

Technology enriches our lives in many incredible ways, yet it also diminishes the human contact we all need. The very devices that are supposed to simplify life often complicate things by placing even more demands on our time and attention. Instead of freeing us, technology can actually weigh us down with the heavy burden of trying to keep up with it all.

Just as Satan tricked Eve with his half-truth about eating the fruit and becoming as wise as God (Genesis 3:4, 5), he deceives us with a partial truth about how technology betters our lives. Undoubtedly, we all benefit from various forms of technology: the convenience it affords, the availability of information at our fingertips, the opportunity for some people to work at home.

These are wonderful advancements. But just as Adam and Eve's knowledge of good and evil came at a price, technological advances have their price too.

By surrounding ourselves with all the latest electronic gadgets and gizmos, we think we will be more connected to those around us and more in touch with the world around us. In reality, we're more disconnected than ever. We believe our lives will be simpler and less stressful, yet actually we have more stress as we deal with information overload. We take pride in being in control of our lives, yet the speed at which technology advances makes us feel more out of control than ever before.

That's the technology trap—and many of us fall for it with very little coaxing.

In reality, we're more disconnected than ever.

Like the other forms of clutter our enemy uses against us, technology has the potential to bring about both great good and great harm. Technology itself is not the problem. Allowing it to take over is the problem. The harm comes when technological advances reach the point of excess and no longer deliver high value to our lives when compared to the high cost of keeping up with them, practically as well as financially. The challenge is knowing how and when to draw the line so technology doesn't become clutter in the first place.

What Would Jesus Do?

The writer of Ecclesiastes didn't know anything about wireless communication or high-speed Internet access, but he did know how easily advances can become setbacks. Ecclesiastes 5:11 says, "As goods increase, so do those who consume them. And what benefit are they to the owner except to feast his eyes on them?" Or as another translation puts it: "The more loot you get, the more looters show up. And what fun is that—to be robbed in broad daylight?" (*The Message*). The more technology we become dependent on, the more effort and expense is required from us to handle it all. With all the stimulation of phones ringing, headphones blaring, microwaves beeping, and inboxes filling with messages, no wonder we can barely hear God when he tries to get our attention!

The writer of Ecclesiastes didn't know anything about wireless communication or high-speed Internet access, but he did know how easily advances can become setbacks.

Remember the last part of the Clarity Principle: "Let us fix our eyes on Jesus." This is the key to using technology to our advantage without being swallowed up by it. We need to learn to think and act like Jesus. If Jesus lived in the twenty-first century, do you think he'd have a cell phone or PDA? Would he have a Web site? I think he would if doing so helped him use his time more wisely and made him more accessible to the people he wanted to reach. I believe Jesus would use all the technology at his disposal, but never, ever let it distract him from his purpose. I am confident Jesus would turn off his cell phone to spend quality time with his family and friends. And I'm willing to bet he could go for days without checking his e-mail—and he wouldn't experience withdrawal. In short, I think Jesus wouldn't let anything electronic stand in the way of what mattered most—loving God and loving people.

My friend Christy used to be the afternoon crossing guard at an elementary school. She shared her sad observation that at least half the parents who picked up their children each afternoon were talking on their cell phones as they drove away from the school with their children. "That is prime time to reconnect with the kids after the day apart," Christy said. "Even if nothing of consequence is shared, the child knows that the parent's focus is on him, at least for a few minutes." But these multitasking parents were forfeiting that opportunity. Whatever benefit they gained by getting something done over the phone, they lost by sending a very clear message about what was most important to them, and they risked the alienation of their children.

I think Jesus wouldn't let anything electronic stand in the way of what mattered most—loving God and loving people.

A major component of living with clarity is learning to use God's gifts for his glory. Technology is a gift, but how you employ it is up to you.

TEMPERING TECHNOLOGY INTRUSION

Although I am behind the times technologically, my husband Michael is a little more out there. A couple of years ago, he broke down and bought a PDA for use in his business. This handheld computer has been a great blessing in helping Michael expand his business, but it has caused its share of arguments at home. More than once on a date night, I've given Michael the you're-in-big-trouble look and griped, "Please put it away!"

One interesting thing that has come from Michael's owning a PDA is that our communication has become more efficient.

Now I know exactly how to get through to him if I need to tell him something important. Because he checks his inbox a hundred times a day, I know that unless my message is lost in cyberspace, he'll get it and usually respond right away. Our friends think it's hysterical that our desks are less than six feet apart, yet we communicate so many of life's details via e-mail.

Often I've wondered whether we have learned to use technology in our favor or have just gotten lazy. Is this an example of finding our best communication style or merely taking the path of least resistance? If we continue communicating so much electronically, will we eventually lose our ability to relate face-to-face?

Have you wondered whether modern technology—e-mail, the Internet, cell phones, whatever—is doing your family more harm than good? Here is a three-part test to help you determine how much technology is too much:

DOES THE TECHNOLOGY I USE DRAW ME CLOSER TO OR PULL ME FURTHER AWAY FROM GOD AND MY LOVED ONES? Sometimes a woman may intend her use of technology to create more time for family and God, but she simply finds herself caught up in the logistics of it all. The bottom line is whether using the technology paves the way or gets in the way of our relationships. Anything that truly encourages communication and quality time together is a relationship builder. Anything that interrupts communication and hinders family time is a relationship barrier.

DOES THE TECHNOLOGY I USE TRULY ENRICH MY LIFE OR ONLY ADD TO CLUTTER? Remember, one definition of clutter is anything that doesn't work for you or add value to your life as it once did. Searching the Web for needed information is productive, but surfing the Web can become a mindless habit.

Conveniences that once seemed beneficial can eventually become a huge drain on your resources. Be objective as you look for signs that technology that you once found helpful no longer gives back as much as it takes.

DOES USING THIS TECHNOLOGY GIVE ME MORE OR LESS TIME FOR WHAT IS MOST IMPORTANT IN MY LIFE? Modern gizmos can both save time and eat it up. Using the Internet is a wonderful way to find information you need, but it can also be a huge time-waster if you don't set limits for its use. The same goes for e-mail and cell phones—they can make life simpler, or they can make life more chaotic if not used with discretion. Think about the time you spend with these conveniences. How much of that time is necessary? And how much would be better spent in talking with your spouse, playing with your kids, or having quiet time alone with God?

Anything that truly encourages communication and quality time together is a relationship builder. Anything that interrupts communication and hinders family time is a relationship barrier.

As you work through these questions, ask God for wisdom and discernment. Invite him to reveal ways in which you may have inadvertently let technology get the upper hand. The goal is not to throw technology away altogether and go back to the Stone Age. You simply want to set limits so that it doesn't take over your life. If you ask, God will help you do that.

Do you feel as if you are in slavery to electronic devices and modern gadgetry? Do you need to pull the plug on technology overload? If so, it's time to clarify and stop the madness. Lighten the load of this clutter, and control the use of technology so it no longer controls you.

CLUTTER *BUSTERS*

◆ What one electronic device could you not live without? Why?

◆ What are some ways that technology you thought would simplify your life has actually complicated life by placing even more demands on your time and energy?

◆ How connected do you feel you need to be? Why? Do you need to set some boundaries to control when and where you can be reached, or when and where you connect with others?

COMING INTO CLARITY

Not long ago I realized that checking my e-mail was taking so long every day, it was becoming a problem for me. So I tackled the issue. First, I got rid of one of my free e-mail addresses because it received so much junk mail, I always spent several minutes each day deleting the junk. Next, I unsubscribed from all the advertising e-mail I receive. Then I unsubscribed from each e-mail newsletter that I didn't get anything useful out of. This was hard because I truly enjoyed reading some of them. I ended up keeping only two. Now my e-mail takes about five minutes to check, and I have more time to spend on the personal e-mails that keep me in touch with long-distance friends.

Lately, I am so much more aware of the time I am spending using the Internet. I pride myself on not watching TV, but the Internet can be just as bad. This is much harder for me to address because I enjoy the Internet, while I've never really liked TV much. But now I refuse to spend precious hours mindlessly surfing the Internet. My reward has been more time to do the things I really love, like being with my kids, being outside, and reading.

Annie
Rib Lake, Wisconsin

TWELVE

GOOD-BYE, CLUTTER!
I've had my fill of needing more! I'm ready to learn to recognize and live with enough.

---

more is never enough

When I was young, some of my favorite TV shows were the old *I Love Lucy* reruns. I was always fascinated by the crazy predicaments Lucy got herself into, and I loved the way she was always quick to come up with a plan, even if it was harebrained and destined to fail.

To this day, one of my favorite episodes is the one in which Lucy tries to bake a loaf of bread from scratch. Even before the bread is done, Lucy's friend Ethel suspects something is wrong when Lucy says she had to go to several stores to buy enough yeast.

"Why? How many cakes of yeast did you need?" Ethel asks.

When Lucy replies, "Thirteen," Ethel knows without a doubt something is wrong. When she looks at the recipe book and points out Lucy's error, Lucy isn't concerned.

"Oh well. They were small," she says casually. "It won't make much difference."

But when Lucy opens the oven to check the bread, she quickly learns that it *did* make a difference! I'll never forget the look on Lucy's face as an eight-foot-long loaf shoots out the oven door and pins her against the kitchen cabinets on the other side of the room.

A fine line exists between need and excess.
That line is called enough.

I can relate to Lucy. I've had my share of comical kitchen mishaps resulting from a lack of discretion in determining how much was enough. Take, for example, the time I was heavy-handed with a highly concentrated dishwasher detergent. Thirty minutes later, my kitchen floor was covered with a thick ooze of suds.

It doesn't matter whether the result is a sudsy mess on the kitchen floor or bread the size of a birch tree; the principle is the same. We all seem to have the inherent belief that more is always better. Why go for a regular hamburger and fries when you can order a triple-deluxe burger combo? Why have one or two designer trinkets when you can have the whole collection? This constant craving for more gets us in trouble every time.

Do the words *more, bigger,* and *better* make frequent appearances in your speech? Even if you don't dwell on making bigger and better purchases, deep down do you believe that having more— more of whatever pushes your hot button—would somehow bring greater enjoyment to your life? We live in an age of acquisition. Somehow we believe that the more we own, the more satisfying our lives will be. The more things we have, we think, the more we will enjoy them all.

In reality, a fine line exists between need and excess. That line is called *enough*, and it is at that point that we find maximum gratification. Once we go past enough, more doesn't bring additional pleasure—only additional heartaches and trouble.

Learning to clarify means learning to find and be comfortable in your state of "enoughness."

THE SIMPLICITY of ENOUGH

My husband has a friend in Virginia who is a self-made millionaire. This man made his fortune by finding a way to profit from the mentality of *more* so prevalent among Americans.

Those of us who try to live with clarity can still be lured into the more mind-set.

In the early 1980s, Mr. Smith owned a large piece of property on the outskirts of his hometown. While looking for a lucrative way to use the land, he came up with what was at the time a novel idea: he built a small tin building and began renting it out as storage space. Soon his business grew, and he added more buildings. By the time Michael met him several years later, Mr. Smith's entire acreage was covered with storage units, and he was one wealthy man!

Sadly, many people live their whole lives in constant pursuit of more and more things—even if it means renting storage facilities to hold it all. Those of us who try to live with clarity can still be lured into the *more* mind-set. Our enemy is a master at devising traps to clutter our lives, and this fascination with more is one of his classics.

Satan knows that if he can keep us occupied with the pursuit of more, we will be distracted from appreciating what we already have. He also knows that having too much keeps us running after the wrong thing. We don't need more possessions to make us happy—what we need is to find greater joy in the things we already have. We don't need more space to hold all we own—what we need is to weed through our belongings, pare down to what truly brings pleasure, and toss the excess.

My friend Amy loves chocolate. (Don't we all?) But here's the difference between Amy and me: If I didn't have to worry about my weight, I would eat a candy bar every day. Not Amy. "I will pay four dollars for one dark chocolate bar from France and make it last a week," she told me once, "rather than buy seven inexpensive candy bars for the same amount and have an entire bar each day."

God doesn't want us to live in the chaos of being burdened with more than we can enjoy.

Amy knows that eating small quantities of fine chocolate satisfies her cravings much better than eating an inexpensive chocolate bar each day. The writer of Proverbs understood this: "Do you like honey? Don't eat too much, or it will make you sick!" (Proverbs 25:16, *NLT*). Or as another translation puts it: "If you find honey, eat just enough—too much of it, and you will vomit." Just enough to fill your needs. Just enough to satisfy your hunger. Just enough to savor but not enough to nauseate. Honey is a wonderful treat, but if you overindulge, you will soon have to deal with unpleasant consequences.

In his goodness, God provides all kinds of pleasures. He also gladly gives us wisdom if we are open to it (James 1:5), which we can use to discern when enough is enough. Too much of anything causes weight gain—not just the physical kind but the emotional and spiritual weight of excess. God does not want our lives cluttered by constantly chasing after more. He doesn't want us to live in the chaos of being burdened with more than we can enjoy.

I met a woman who appeared on the reality TV show *Wife Swap*. For two weeks, Kathy switched places with another woman whose lifestyle was very different from hers. A devout Christian who homeschools all eight of her children, Kathy lives very simply and frugally with her family. When interviewed prior to the show, Kathy told the producers, "Material things are only here for a short time, and they are not important."

For the swap, Kathy was paired up with a compulsive shopper who spends sixty thousand dollars a year keeping up with the latest fashion trends. In contrast to Kathy's conservative approach, this woman told producers her life motto is: More, more, more.

"She had to shop all the time because she would only wear her clothes one time, and then she got rid of them," Kathy recalls. "This meant she had to work all the time to pay for her lifestyle."

When Kathy moved into her temporary home, she quickly saw that the family was starved for attention. The woman with the constant quest for more of life's luxuries had driven a wedge between herself and her family. The family loved how much time Kathy spent talking with them, and when the two-week swap was over, they actually seemed sad to see Kathy go.

THE DIFFERENCE BETWEEN ENOUGH and EXCESS

Our Father's desire is for us to revel in the freedom and simplicity of enough (see Matthew 6:19-21 and 1 Timothy 6:6-8). To do that, we must trust his provision and learn the difference between enough and excess. The first part of the Clarity Principle tells us to "throw off everything that hinders." The mind-set of wanting more is a hindrance because it lures us to step out of the safety and security of trusting God's provision and into the oppression of overload.

When I lived a year in Japan, my life was the epitome of clarity and simplicity. I didn't have a car—a bicycle took me anywhere I needed to go. I didn't have many clothes—just what I carried across the Pacific in two large suitcases. My apartment was small—smaller than the bonus room of the house Michael and I now own. By American standards, I didn't have much, but I had all I needed. No clutter, no space issues, no wondering what to do with all my things.

> *Our Father's desire is for us to revel in the freedom and simplicity of enough.*

Fast forward to my life ten years later. The year was 2003, and my first book had just been published. To promote the book, I was doing quite a bit of speaking around the country. I wanted to look nice for these engagements, so I began to fret over my clothes. There was hardly any empty space in my closet, yet I thought I didn't have a thing to wear! I began asking God to provide more clothes.

Well, the Lord answered my prayers, but not as I expected. Instead of giving me a new wardrobe, he made it clear: "Nancy, you don't need more clothes. What you need is to learn to use the ones you have."

Not exactly the response I was looking for! Yet it was the one I needed to hear. How could I have gone from being comfortable with so little in Japan to being so acquisitions-minded in the US? This incident began a process of attitude adjustment that lasted several years.

DEALING with I-SEE-IT-I-WANT-IT

The lust for more seems to be an inevitable part of life on this earth (see 1 John 2:16), but using the following steps, you can learn to derail this form of lifestyle clutter.

One great strategy is to develop the habit of getting rid of one old thing for every new thing you bring home.

TAKE TIME TO ASSESS YOUR ATTITUDE. You must be sick enough of the status quo to say "I'm not going to live this way any longer." You have to be fed up with living in a cluttered home, fed up with wasting your money on things that bring little joy. You have to be sick and tired of your excess making you sick and tired! Let your anger and disgust over the situation propel you to action.

DISCARD OLD HABITS, AND DEVELOP NEW ONES TO REPLACE THE OLD. Once you are determined to change, then you have to develop some new habits to replace the I-see-it-I-want-it routine. One great strategy is to develop the habit of getting rid of one old thing for every new thing you bring home. This forces you to think about how much you really want the new item. While you're thinking about which old item to get rid of, think through the consequences and the costs involved with buying the new item. Ask yourself: Where exactly am I going to put this? How often will I use it? Will acquiring this item actually solve a particular problem or only create another problem—such as overcrowding in my home or a balance on my credit card that I can't pay? What will this item cost me in terms of cleaning, maintenance, and space in my home?

PURCHASE WITH CAUTION. Another good habit is to insist on a cooling-off period—a day, a week, or even a month—before making any purchase. This will give you time to think through the above questions. Don't let the excitement of the moment or the fear of missing out on a good deal cause you to rush into something you'll regret. If a potential purchase can't stand up to the scrutiny of careful consideration, that's a good indication you don't need the item anyway.

ASK FOR HELP. Ask God to teach you how to recognize and enjoy your state of "enoughness." Ask him to take away your need to acquire. Request that he replace that need with an openness to receive what he has for you and an appreciation for what he has already provided. Enlist other people in your efforts too. Find another woman who understands the principle of enough and ask her to mentor you.

Are you ready to let go of excess so you can embrace *enough*? Are you eager to experience the maximum gratification that comes from having just enough? Let go of the *more* mentality for good. If you do, you will be able to experience clarity unlike anything you've ever experienced before.

◉ CLUTTER *BUSTERS* ◉

◆ What do you think about the concept of *enough*? Do you know when you are dangerously close to crossing the line between need and excess? What warning signals do you recognize?

◆ Do you have any humorous personal stories about "a little more" turning out to be way too much? What can we learn about human nature from these experiences?

◆ Think about this statement: "We don't need more possessions to make us happy—what we need is to find greater joy in the things we already have." How would applying this thought make your life more enjoyable and less stressful?

◆ Who do you know who could mentor you in this area of living with enough? Plan to contact that person and discuss this.

COMING INTO CLARITY

When my husband and I first got married, we had no credit cards, almost no money, and only one car. People said we could never make it on what my husband made, but somehow we did. A few weeks ago, I drove back to our old Atlanta neighborhood and looked around.

I cried as I remembered the wonderful times we had in that house. We didn't know we didn't have much money, and we didn't know we were supposed to be unhappy about it. I was pregnant one hot Georgia summer with no air conditioning. We didn't have central heat either. We played outside all the time, raking up leaves in the fall and then jumping in them all day, and sliding down the icy church parking lot on trash can lids in the winter.

Those were the days—before the conveniences of digital TV, cable, computers, and cell phones. Now we have all of that plus some, and yet we have less time to spend with our families. What happened? We work all the time to have more material things. Having all these things has not made our lives better, but worse in many ways. All of us, including me, need to learn from this.

Brenda
Peachtree City, Georgia

from cluttered
money matters
to financial
clarity

Wisdom or money can get you almost anything,

but it's important to know that only wisdom

can save your life.

ECCLESIASTES 7:12 (*NLT*)

Watch yourselves! Keep from wanting all kinds

of things you should not have. A man's life is not

made up of things, even if he has many riches.

LUKE 12:15 (*NLV*)

THIRTEEN

GOOD-BYE, CLUTTER!

I'm done with feeling deprived. I'm learning how to appreciate simple pleasures and enjoy life regardless of my income.

---

living the good life

*H*ow many children do you know who would turn down a cookie before dinner?

Lydia's friend Leon and his dad were visiting us. While Michael and Leon's dad were talking out in the yard, Lydia came inside with Leon to ask if they could each have one of the cookies I had baked. Normally I say no to cookies before dinner, but that day I relented. Lydia took two cookies from the plate and started to hand one to Leon.

"No," Leon said. "I don't want it."

Turn down one of my special cookies? I thought. *This child must be sick!*

"I don't want the small one," he argued. "I want the big one!" Then I understood the reason for Leon's strange behavior.

Lydia didn't want to give away the bigger cookie and keep the smaller one for herself. Leon didn't want the smaller cookie when Lydia's larger one looked so much more appealing. I'm sure that Leon normally would have been appreciative of receiving a cookie before dinner, but because he compared his cookie to Lydia's, he wasn't satisfied. He continued to feel deprived until I took a big bite of Lydia's cookie to make it the same size as his!

Aren't we all like Leon at times? Instead of appreciating everything we have, we compare it to what others have. Instead of being thankful for all our blessings, we stack them up against others' blessings to see how ours rank. Inevitably, when we do this, we feel deprived, as Leon did.

The same situation can look completely different, depending on the mind-set through which you choose to filter it.

Do you sometimes feel cheated because you can't afford to spend as much as your friends or neighbors? Do you think it's not fair that you work just as hard as others but don't seem to have as much to show for it? Do you feel that what you have is nice, but not quite as nice as what someone else has?

Living well is a state of mind, and so is living with feelings of deprivation. We can freely choose between the two.

Living the good life is not some exclusive privilege reserved only for the rich and famous. Living well is not about how much you have, but about how much you appreciate and enjoy what you have.

A MATTER of PERSPECTIVE

Are you rich or poor? Comfortable or barely scraping by? It's all a matter of perspective. Several years ago, subscribers to my newsletter discussed the issue of feeling deprived when your financial situation requires you to live frugally. Several subscribers wrote to say that you can't always choose your financial circumstances but you can choose what attitude you will take toward those circumstances. One reader came up with an interesting scenario to illustrate how the same situation can look completely different, depending on the mind-set through which you choose to filter it:

> Pretend you come to my house for dinner, and this is what I serve: a huge pot of black-eyed peas cooked with a ham hock, a large pan of thick, sweet southern cornbread, and a cast-iron skillet full of greens you don't recognize. I tell you the greens are dandelion greens I picked this morning and wilted with some bacon grease left over from breakfast.

> What if this hypothetical meal also included your choice of iced tea or water to drink and blackberry cobbler for dessert? Let's say I made the cobbler from scratch with blackberries picked free from wild blackberry bushes growing by the side of the road. Depending on your viewpoint, you would form an opinion about whether I was living well or not.

> You may look at this meal and think that I am poor because I'm eating roadside blackberries and yard weeds. Or you might look at it and think that I'm doing quite well because I can afford a ham hock in my beans and had bacon for breakfast.

Same situation, two different interpretations. Your attitude about the situation determines whether you define it as living well or living in deprivation.

THE COMPARISON TRAP

On days when Lydia is dangerously close to getting on my last nerve, I've been known to jokingly say, "Are you trying to be irritating, or is it just working out that way?" She may not mean to be annoying by playing loudly or chattering nonstop, but at that moment she is, nonetheless.

Satan knows that judging one's quality of life by the standards of others is never beneficial.

In the same way, most of us don't intentionally set out to be ungrateful. We know how richly we have been blessed. We know how comfortable our lives are when compared to many others in the world. And we also know that no matter what challenges we face, things could always be worse. Yet we are still more prone to dwell on the way things could be rather than give thanks for the way things *are*.

Why does this happen? Believe me, it doesn't happen by accident. Our adversary works very hard at influencing our perception of living well. He is a master at luring us into focusing only on material blessings, ignoring all the other things God so graciously gives. Our natural fascination with comparison is a powerful weapon he uses for stirring up feelings of discontent. He knows that judging one's quality of life by the standards of others is never beneficial. It's always self-defeating because we can always find someone better off than ourselves.

A woman I met had learned firsthand the dangers of comparing her financial situation to that of others. Early in her marriage, Lisa harbored negative feelings about not having much money. She often looked at families that were more financially secure than hers, and she felt resentful. This negativity continued for several years until she realized it wasn't healthy. Then she decided to take a different approach.

Instead of dwelling on how little her family had, Lisa made a list of all the things for which they could be thankful. They had a roof over their heads. The family car ran dependably. They were all in good health. Lisa was able to stay home with her children. As she wrote down each thing that came to mind, the list grew quite long. When she finished, she looked at the list and realized that instead of being poor, her family was richly blessed.

Lisa's story illustrates an important principle. The person living on ten thousand dollars a year could easily feel deprived—if she chooses to do so—because she can't live and spend like the person making twenty-five thousand. The person living on twenty-five thousand a year could feel deprived because she can't live like the person making fifty thousand. The person living on fifty thousand a year could feel deprived too, because she can't live like the person making six figures. As long as we base our internal feelings of satisfaction on external factors—how our life circumstances stack up to those whose circumstances seem better—we will always end up feeling deprived and depressed.

Unless we learn to live the good life on a smaller income, a larger income will never be large enough.

RESTING in GOD's GOODNESS

When you hear talk about "the good life," what comes to mind? A new car every two years? A spacious home in a well-to-do neighborhood? Fortunately for us, God's definition of the good life is much better than that. It's something we all can have—something we already have, whether we realize it or not. The good life is simply a life showered with God's goodness.

Psalm 116:7 says, "Be at rest once more, O my soul, for the LORD has been good to you." Regardless of your income or social status, God has showered and will continue to shower his goodness on you again and again. You don't have to fret if your cookie doesn't seem as big as someone else's. You can rest in thankfulness and appreciation for what you do have, knowing that God has been good to you.

On some level, this tendency to define the good life by worldly standards is a hindrance that entices us all. How easy it is to get caught up in unhealthy comparisons. But remember what the first part of the Clarity Principle tells us: "Let us throw off everything that hinders and the sin that so easily entangles." Ingratitude is a grievous sin when it causes us to look at our lives through deprivation-colored glasses. But when we change our perspective on what it means to live well, we soon realize that nothing stands in the way of our living the good life—no income shortage, no financial hardship, nothing—except our own attitude toward whatever circumstances we face.

Have you ever noticed that those times of having few financial resources can actually be some of the best times of your life? A few years ago I asked several friends if they could think of a time in their own lives when they didn't have much money but fully enjoyed everything they had. The variety of answers these women shared was heartwarming.

Amiel talked about the hard times she and her husband faced when they first married: "In the beginning of our marriage, we had several occasions when we were counting pennies just to survive between paydays. Instead of those being depressing years, we grew closer to each other."

Mary Ann remembered when her husband was attending school full-time: "Our oldest daughter was seven months old, and we had no insurance or benefits. It was such a special time to live the simple life and just enjoy spending time with my daughter."

Yvonne thought back to a time when she went through a major life transition: "I lived in a month-to-month apartment with just the bare basics. I had a small TV, two lawn chairs, and a mattress and box spring with no frame. I used the boxes I moved in with as my dresser, nightstand, coffee table, and dinner table. I had nothing except freedom, and I felt great."

Financially, these women were poor, but they didn't feel poor because they focused not on their lack, but on their abundance. They lived well because they chose to live well—not comparing themselves with others but reveling in what God had given them.

CULTIVATING a GRATEFUL HEART

Michael and I have experienced our share of having very little. Most times we have chosen, as my friends did, to view our cup as half full rather than half empty. But I can remember a season when I struggled with this. It was during the Christmas holidays right before Lydia was born. Our businesses had not done well that year, and with the added expenses of a pregnancy without insurance coverage, our budget was even tighter than usual by the time the holidays rolled around.

"I wish Christmas would just go away!" I told Michael in a moment of frustration as we talked about whether we should buy a Christmas tree that year. We could barely afford inexpensive presents for everyone on our list; how could we justify spending even fifteen to twenty dollars more for a small tree?

I felt poor, and I didn't like the feeling. Intellectually, I knew Christmas was not about how much we could spend or whether we had elaborate decorations. I also knew we had more than our share to be thankful for—not the least of which was a beautiful baby on the way. Yet in my heart I couldn't shake the feeling of being deprived because our holiday celebration would be much simpler than that of our relatives and friends.

Have you ever experienced a similar situation? Are you feeling that life has dealt you a bad hand compared with that of someone else? Here are some things I did that you can also do to help move from feeling sorry for yourself to feeling grateful within your circumstances:

REFOCUS ON YOUR BLESSINGS. Although we couldn't afford expensive gifts, we could afford to give each person on our list something. Although we couldn't buy a tree, we had an ample supply of decorations to make the house look festive. What can you be thankful for in your current circumstances? Instead of focusing on what isn't as you'd like it to be, focus on the blessings to be found when you choose to look for them.

PUT YOUR CREATIVITY TO WORK. I worked hard at finding out-of-the-ordinary ways for us to give of ourselves while still giving within our means. Instead of feeling bad because I couldn't buy expensive gifts, I focused on using my time and talents to express my love for each person on my list. Likewise, you will probably feel much better about your situation if you approach it with a healthy dose of creativity. Look for ways to enjoy simple pleasures and make the most of what you have.

LET GO OF PRECONCEIVED EXPECTATIONS AND IDEAS. Having a good Christmas that year required that I let go of any expectations about what an enjoyable holiday celebration was supposed to be. I knew that if I busied myself with being thankful and resourceful, there wouldn't be much time left for feeling sorry for myself. You too may have to let go of some preconceived notions about what it means for you and your family to have a satisfying life. Ask God to help you let go of worldly definitions of success and accomplishment so you can embrace his definition of living the good life.

Has the habit of comparison held you back? Have you allowed ingratitude to sneak in and steal your joy? If so, it's time to get rid of any faulty perceptions of what it means to live well. Choose instead to live with gratitude, and rest in the clarity of God's goodness.

CLUTTER *BUSTERS*

◆ In the past, when you've heard someone talk about "the good life," what images came to mind? Has your opinion of what constitutes the good life changed?

◆ Think about this statement: "Unless we learn to live the good life on a smaller income, a larger income will never be large enough." Do you agree or disagree? Why?

◆ Do you agree that nothing stands between you and the good life except your own attitude toward your situation? What about people who live in true poverty? Can their choice of attitude make their poverty bearable?

COMING INTO CLARITY

We are members of a church located in the midst of half-million-dollar homes. Many of our church members live in these homes; we do not. Sometimes I feel a little envious when I see my friends' huge houses with professionally decorated rooms that look like magazine photos. But whenever I start feeling this way, I remind myself of all the blessings I have.

I am fortunate to be a stay-at-home wife. I have a lovely little home that is just right for my husband and me and our two cats. Several people on different occasions have walked into my home and commented that it is so peaceful. That one word really sums up what it's all about. My home may not be big, it may not be professionally decorated or magazine worthy, but there is peace within. We have everything we need. I remind myself that we are positively wealthy compared to the majority of the world. This never fails to drive away those feelings of discontent.

Anne
Dallas, Texas

FOURTEEN

GOOD-BYE, CLUTTER!
Enough with careless spending and sporadic saving! I am tired of living my financial life for the moment.

stewardship is more than giving

Around the time Lydia reached the ripe old age of four, Michael and I decided it was time for her to begin learning the cold, hard facts of life. Her education began with an introduction to this rule: If you want to buy something, you have to save your money to get it.

Lydia had her eye on a super-duper self-rewinding yo-yo, and we decided this was the perfect opportunity to teach Lydia about saving. Michael first took her to the store to find out exactly how much it cost: $3.99 plus tax. Then they came home, and together they made a chart to track her progress as she saved toward her goal.

"OK, Lydia," Michael said when the chart was done. "Let's see how much money you have so we can write it on your chart."

Lydia had various stashes of cash around the house. First, we emptied the wooden bank her grandfather had made for her, then the pink piggy bank she got for Christmas. Then all the various change purses she owned. Before we knew it, we had an impressive mound of moola on the floor in front of us. Most of it was pennies, but it was impressive nonetheless.

Good stewardship is simply seeing your money as a gift from God and showing your appreciation by taking care of it and using it wisely.

When we counted and rolled all the coins, we were stunned to find that Lydia had more than enough. Her ten cents here and twenty-five cents there seemed insignificant, but when added together it was a significant amount—enough for Lydia and Michael to go back to the store and purchase her yo-yo that very day.

Many years ago Ben Franklin said, "Beware of little expenses. A small leak will sink a great ship."[1] We tend to dismiss small amounts of money because we feel they are unimportant, thinking that ten or twenty or even a hundred dollars here or there makes no difference. But what we fail to see is that when we fritter away what seems a minor sum now, we forfeit the chance to do something even more worthy with that money later.

Does it always seem that the money you want to save, invest, or give ends up being spent on other things first? Regardless of how much money you earn, you will—if you're like most people—always find a way to spend it all unless you make a conscious effort to do otherwise. Good stewardship is simply seeing your money as a gift from God and showing your appreciation by taking care of it and using it wisely.

THE BIG DEAL ABOUT LITTLE THINGS

Good money management is not something that happens by accident. It requires diligence and persistence in watching over the details.

Several years ago I chatted with Carrie, who had been married for less than a year. In the months since her wedding, Carrie and her husband had racked up five thousand dollars in credit card debt. "The bad part about it is that I can't even tell you where it all went," she added. Carrie could recall a few of the larger items purchased with the credit card, but most of the debt was for purchases so insignificant she couldn't even remember what they were! All those minor purchases added up to a major burden of debt for this young couple.

Satan loves keeping us focused on the little picture (our short-term wants and needs) so we don't see the big picture (our long-term financial health and stability).

What happened to Carrie and her husband is not uncommon. Our enemy leads us to believe that the little details of our financial lives are no big deal. It's all part of the enemy's scheme for making sure we are too distracted to be intentional about how we manage our money. Satan loves keeping us focused on the little picture (our short-term wants and needs) so we don't see the big picture (our long-term financial health and stability). In focusing only on the here and now, not only do we endanger our own financial future, we also hamper our ability to use our financial blessings to help others.

Since day one of our marriage, Michael has been adamant about saving regularly for retirement. Even at times when our income has been sparse, he has always insisted that we set aside at least 10 percent. That's why we've also made it our policy to always have a budget and avoid debt. We know we won't be able to save for the future unless we control our spending and live within our means now.

Being careless in the small things keeps us from being careful in the big things.

If you ask Michael why he feels so strongly about saving for retirement, he explains it this way: "If you don't pay your car payment, the bank takes away your car. If you don't pay your mortgage, the mortgage company takes away your house. But if you don't pay yourself by saving for your retirement, you take away your own future."

Take away your own future? Your family's future? That sounds harsh, but that is exactly what many of us do by not being deliberate in handling our money. Being careless in the small things keeps us from being careful in the big things. The result is that we don't have the money to do what's truly important because we let it slip away.

Make Mine "Well Done"

Jesus told a story about a master who gave three of his servants some money to handle while he was on a long trip (see Matthew 25:14-30). The master didn't give each servant the same amount of money, but he did have the same expectation for all three: they were to use the money wisely until he returned.

When it was time for the servants to give a report on how they had handled the money, two of them had good news for their master. By making wise choices, each had doubled the amount he was originally given. But the third servant's report was not as encouraging. Because of his own insecurity and irresponsibility, he had kept his money safely hidden. As we look at how the master commended the first two servants, we learn what God expects from us: "Well done, good and faithful servant! You have been faithful with a few things; I will put you in charge of many things. Come and share your master's happiness!" (Matthew 25:21). God has given us all gifts and blessings—but not all the same gifts and blessings, and not in the same proportions. It brings God joy to see us use his endowments in ways that express our reverence and gratitude for what we have been given. And as we are trustworthy in taking care of the small matters, we prove that we can be trusted with even more of God's blessings.

STEWARDSHIP IS MORE THAN GIVING

What pastors and other church leaders usually mean when they talk about stewardship is giving. But don't assume that's all there is to it. Stewardship is just as much about *living* as it is about *giving*. Good stewardship is about being faithful in using all your resources—not only your money and possessions but your time and talent as well. Stewardship is a duty, but it is also an act of worship (see 2 Corinthians 8:1-5 and Philippians 4:18). How can we look at all that God has poured out into our lives and not want to use those things to please him?

Because Christians have experienced so much of God's love and grace, you'd think we would be the most conscientious people around when it comes to managing money, yet this is not always the case. A couple of years ago, I was part of a discussion about stewardship and how Christians practice it today. Several women in the group made interesting observations.

"Based on what I have seen, I don't believe most Christians are faithful in the little things in regard to finances," Angel commented. "It is often hard to tell the believers from the nonbelievers, based on their giving and money management. Many do not seem willing to help out fellow Christians in need other than to say 'I will pray for you.'"

"I am often disheartened by the display of Christians in regard to sharing and managing our finances," Amiel added. "If there is a food drive or clothing drive, there are many of us who participate, but what food do we contribute? What clothing is given? Often it is the cheapest of store brands, clothing that is far outdated, and toys that have missing pieces or are dirty."

Another woman, whose husband is a minister in one of the largest denominations in the country, observed that most churches pay their ministers so poorly that church members could never live on those salaries themselves. The churches do this with the assumption that the wife will work to supplement the family income. This makes it extremely difficult for pastors who want their wives to stay home with the children. This woman said that she and her husband often see church members "blow fifty dollars on a meal" and not think anything of it, something the church's pastors can never do. Not only do some members spend carelessly, they also make poor choices for their families as they pursue bigger homes and more possessions. This woman said she couldn't help but feel frustrated at times to see Christians show so little concern for how they manage their blessings.

"Let us run with perseverance the race marked out for us." This part of the Clarity Principle sheds light on what we have been called to in handling the resources God bestows. Like other forms of clutter, careless money management complicates life by bringing chaos and confusion to our financial affairs. We can quickly lose sight of what it means to respond to God's goodness with a posture of gratefulness. But being intentional with our money clarifies life by helping us stay focused on doing the best we can with what we've been given.

GETTING BACK on TRACK

I don't believe any of us means to get sloppy in the small stuff; we just become preoccupied with the demands of life, trading conscientiousness for convenience because we are busy. We let the little details slide a little here and slide a little there and later face a deluge of larger, more complicated issues because of it.

Being intentional with our money clarifies life by helping us stay focused on doing the best we can with what we've been given.

Several years ago, Michael and I were doing very well in budgeting and saving for the future—until we moved, that is. All the expenses involved in moving across the state, selling one home, and buying another threw us off balance. With so many other things on our minds during the transition, we got lax with our money management.

It's OK, we thought. *When we're finally settled, we'll get back on track.*

Then came our wakeup call. Soon after we moved to Knoxville, we learned we were expecting our first child. What a surprise! And what a huge motivation to get back on track fast! We quickly returned to the practice of careful spending and saving.

Just how does someone go from being off track to being on target when it comes to stewardship? Consider these strategies:

DOCUMENT YOUR SPENDING. First, you need to know what your spending habits have been so far. Write down everything you spend for the next month or two. This will show you exactly where your money is going. Then look carefully at your expenditures. Which of these were needs and which were wants? Which expenditures were good and prudent uses of your resources? And which would you have avoided if only you'd thought through the purchase more carefully?

LOOK CAREFULLY AT YOUR SPENDING TRENDS. As you study your spending habits, you should begin to see trends. Does your discretion about spending tend to diminish in certain situations? Is there any particular category—entertainment, clothing, things for your children—for which you seem especially prone to overspending? As you consider the trends you observe, ask God to show you positive steps you can take to be a better steward in the problem areas.

Write down everything you spend for the next month or two.
This will show you exactly where your money is going.

ESTABLISH A SPENDING PLAN. Understand that the point is not to totally deprive yourself or never allow for spontaneity in spending. That's not what good stewardship is all about. The goal is to make sure you put first things first in how you handle your money: giving to God, saving for short-term needs and emergencies that arise, saving for long-term needs like retirement and your children's education. A family budget is the single most important tool for keeping you conscientious about how you spend and deliberate about how you save. If you don't already have one and don't know where to start, see the Resources section at the back of this book for biblically based resources for budgeting.

Are you tired of trading long-term financial stability for short-term convenience and pleasures? Are you ready to bring clarity to how you handle all God has put in your care? If so, make a commitment to say good-bye to the clutter of careless money management so you can begin making stewardship a way of life.

CLUTTER *BUSTERS*

◆ Consider this statement: "Stewardship is just as much about *living* as it is about *giving*." What kind of impact will thinking about stewardship in that way make on your life?

◆ How could truly grasping that your financial resources belong to God change your spending, saving, and giving habits?

◆ Do you agree that having a family budget is an integral part of good stewardship? Do you think it is possible to be careful in day-to-day money management without some sort of budgeting plan? Are you willing to commit to developing and maintaining a budget if you are not doing this already?

COMING INTO CLARITY

I participated in a Bible study about simplicity several years ago. During the study those taking part were encouraged to imagine that our earthly possessions were suddenly destroyed or stolen. We were then challenged to actually sell or give away the item that we would miss the most, in order to free ourselves from materialism and allow God to work in our lives.

An uncle had given me a hope chest for my high school graduation, and it had much sentimental value. Through my twenties, the chest moved with me from apartment to apartment. After I married, it held memories and photo albums and was a centerpiece in our living room. However, I felt God was telling me to let go of it. After prayer and discussion with my husband, we placed an ad in the local paper. I felt very comfortable with the Christian buyer and was able to help two mission organizations with the funds I received from the sale. I have not missed this item because I still have the memory of the day my uncle presented it to me.

Another thing I felt God was asking me to share was a rocker we bought when my son was born. We spent hours searching out the most comfortable rocker. The one we found fit us perfectly and was enjoyed for several years. A couple at church was starting a family, and they were searching for the perfect rocker. Again after prayer and discussion, we decided to give them our chair for use in their family. Though the chair is gone, I still have the memory of rocking my son to sleep.

Through the years God has used these experiences to help me remember that all the money and possessions we have are just loans from God. If and when he has a better use for them, we need to let them go and be free to watch God work.

Meg
Union, Iowa

FIFTEEN

GOOD-BYE, CLUTTER!
*Debt, you're outta here! I see through the deception, and I
don't want indebtedness to control me any longer.*

---

sweet freedom

*T*he story of Cinderella is a favorite fairy tale even for adults because it contains two things all women love: a handsome prince and a happy ending.

Sweet and likable, Cinderella was forced to live as a servant to her mean-spirited stepmother and two selfish stepsisters. No matter what she did or how hard she worked, Cinderella could not please her mistresses. Hers was a dreary existence of hard labor and few options for a better life.

Because of her servitude, Cinderella couldn't do the things she really wanted to do. Something as delightful as going to a ball definitely was out of her reach. Cinderella's life was grim until her fairy godmother showed up and made all Cinderella's dreams come true with a wave of her wand. Not only did Cinderella attend the ball, she also met her Prince Charming and was soon whisked away to live happily ever after!

Cinderella's pre-fairy-godmother predicament very

much resembles the situation of many women today, with just one difference. Instead of serving an evil stepmother, these women are enslaved by an equally oppressive taskmaster: debt.

Debt: Friend or Foe?

Like Cinderella, families ruled by debt are limited in their options. Mom wants to homeschool the children? She can't because she has to work full-time to help pay the bills. Dad's job is super stressful? He can't take an easier, lower-paying job because the family needs every bit of his salary. Dreams of starting a business or retiring early are fantasies because of debt.

Do you think you'd have to be on the verge of bankruptcy to be seriously affected by debt? Think again.

Benjamin Franklin had very definite opinions about debt. One of my favorites is "Better to go to bed supperless, than wake up in debt."[1] What a stark contrast to the attitude many have toward debt today. Instead of something to be avoided, we have embraced credit as a friend—an easy way to bypass shortages of funds. If debt was once such a disgrace, why do we now see debt as a strange sort of blessing rather than a curse?

Part of the problem is our cultural mind-set that debt is normal. It's as if you are somehow abnormal if you choose to avoid it. We face a fierce pressure to live as "everyone else" does—even if that means spending beyond our incomes. We want the same standard of living as our parents and grandparents, without all the hard work and saving they did to get where they are.

We've bought into the lie that says living the good life means having what we want when we want it. The line of thinking goes like this: "If you want to be happy, you have to have stuff. To have stuff, you have to have money. If you don't have money, you can still have stuff, but you have to have debt." Debt is seen as a necessary evil.

What Happens When Debt Rules

Do you think you'd have to be on the verge of bankruptcy to be seriously affected by debt? Think again. Debt changes the way we live and the way we relate to our families. Many mothers who would rather stay home with their new babies can't because they have to go back to work. Couples who say that family time is most important rarely see each other and their kids because they must work long hours to make payments on their debt. Decisions are not made according to what is best for the family but, instead, what is necessary to pay basic expenses plus all the debt too.

Have you seen the bumper sticker that says "I owe, I owe, so off to work I go"? Sadly, this slogan seems to be our national anthem. Instead of working just enough to pay for necessities and then using the rest of our time to enjoy life, we spend more than we can afford on things to make life comfortable, then we fill our hours with work to pay for those things.

Does your family have more consumer debt than you care to admit? How would your life look if you were debt free? What would you do that you can't do now? Would you spend more time with your family? Volunteer more? Explore career options that never seemed viable before? Likewise, what wouldn't you do that you must do now? Would being free from financial concerns make it easier to live life the way you truly want to live it? What we gain in possessions and comforts and other niceties purchased on credit, we lose in time—time with God, time with our children and spouses, time to do the things that enrich our lives the most. We also lose control—control over our time, our choices, and our future.

A few years ago an acquaintance shared an interesting story. At the time, Suzy worked for a midsize, family-owned company. Suzy held a management position, so she had an insider's view of the company's inner workings. She noticed that the upper management kept a close eye on the employees' personal financial situations. They knew which families were deeply in debt and those that weren't, and this information influenced how they treated their employees.

Suzy also knew this was true from firsthand experience. When she and her husband were struggling with debt, her supervisors were much more demanding and less accommodating when one of her children was sick or she needed to attend meetings at their school. Once her family had completed a debt-reduction program and was no longer saddled with debt, her supervisors knew she could leave the company anytime she wanted, so they took extra precautions to ensure her job satisfaction.

Like the other forms of clutter Satan uses so skillfully, debt takes your attention away from God.

Suzy's story is a powerful example of how Satan can use debt as a noose around your neck. First, he lures you into the debt trap with lies: "Debt is harmless." "Buying on credit makes life easier." Once you've signed on the dotted line, you quickly see that debt does anything but make your life simple. Whether you owe a little or a lot, being in debt causes you to have divided loyalties. How can you truly put your family first when financial obligations dictate when, where, and how much you work? How can you fully pursue God's will for your life when you are so busy just trying to pay the bills?

Like the other forms of clutter Satan uses so skillfully, debt takes your attention away from God. Buying on credit keeps you from looking to God for his provision to meet your needs. After all, why wait for God to provide when instant credit and no down payment mean you can provide for yourself right away?

WHO ARE YOU SERVING?

Because debt is such an accepted part of our culture, you may be wondering how God feels about your credit rating. Does he really care whether you are in debt? Look at what the Bible says. Proverbs 22:7 tells us, "The borrower is servant to the lender," or as another translation puts it, "Don't borrow and put yourself under [the lender's] power" (The Message). When you acquire debt, you pledge allegiance to your creditors. You become a slave to your lenders, promising to do whatever is necessary to pay them back. God does not want us to be in bondage to anything or anyone. He wants us to be free to serve him without limitations and distractions.

Several years ago I met a woman, Leimome, who was interested in learning to live a more simple, uncluttered life. "I believe God is calling me to do something different with my life," she said. "I feel like he keeps saying, 'Pack your bags; get ready to go.'"

Leimome didn't know exactly what God had in mind for her. But whatever it was, she was sure of this: when God's plans became clear, she did not want anything holding her back. Part of her plan for "packing her bags" was to pay off all of her remaining debt as soon as possible.

By making freedom from debt a priority, Leimome was practicing the first part of the Clarity Principle: "Let us throw off everything that hinders." She knew that being debt free would make it easier for her to do whatever God called her to do. She didn't want anything hindering her from responding to God's call. Leimome also was practicing the third part of the Clarity Principle: "Let us fix our eyes on Jesus." As a Christian— a servant of Christ—she wanted her life to be ruled by doing *his* work, not whatever work was necessary to repay her debt.

BREAKING FREE

Radio-show host and financial guru Dave Ramsey often talks about money being a wonderful slave but a terrible master. When you put it to work for you, money can perform many wonderful functions: providing for your family, securing a stable financial future, funding charitable causes . . . As long as you are in control, money serves you well. But when you choose to live on credit, everything changes. You abdicate your position of authority over your money and allow it to become the boss.

Adela is a friend who knows what a stranglehold debt can be. Although her family's credit card debt was not as high as that of others they knew, it was daunting to them nonetheless. Even more disheartening was the fact that most of their debt could have been avoided if they had just saved up for their purchases.

To climb out from under this burden, Adela and her husband, Tony, made sacrifices and changed their spending habits. They always paid more than the minimum payment each month, even if they could only afford to pay an additional five dollars. Any rebate or tax returns they received also went toward paying down debt. As they paid off each credit card, they cancelled that card so they wouldn't be tempted to use it again.

"Getting out of debt simplified everything," Adela says, "and what a load it took off our shoulders!" Although Adela and Tony are still working in the same jobs, even their work is more enjoyable now. They are no longer counting the days and minutes until the next payday.

When you choose to live on credit, everything changes.
You abdicate your position of authority over your money
and allow it to become the boss.

"We ponder our purchases in a more spiritual way now," Adela says. "Do we need it? Do we love it? Can we refurbish something we already own to fit our needs? Our possessions are dearer to us when we choose them more carefully and work and save to obtain them. And we are keenly aware that God will provide at the proper time."

Adela's family now enjoys being free from credit card debt. Using these steps, your family can experience that same freedom:

STOP SUGAR-COATING DEBT. You must see debt for what it really is: slavery. Consumer debt is not a necessity. It is not a convenience or a luxury. Debt is a ball and chain that keeps you from living your life the way God wants you want to live it. Get angry about the situation, and use your anger to propel you into action to do something about it.

TAKE RESPONSIBILITY FOR THE PROBLEM. Take a serious look at why those debts occurred. Debt is an external symptom of clutter of the heart. Spend time figuring out what is going on inside you that caused the debt in the first place. Was it because your family didn't trust and wait for God's provision? Did you try to take the easy way out and use credit instead of saving up for what you needed? Even if your debt occurred because of legitimate needs, could you have avoided debt by setting aside funds to cover the inevitable emergencies of life? Whatever the underlying reason for the debt, admit any wrongdoing on your part, and ask God to help you deal with that issue.

Debt is an external symptom of clutter of the heart.

SEEK GODLY COUNSEL. Seek counsel about the best way to deal with your debt. Several Christian organizations specifically help families use biblical principles to break free from debt. See the Resources section at this end of this book for programs that can give the guidance and support you need to work through the steps of debt repayment.

BE PATIENT. Just as we don't gain weight overnight, we don't sink deeply into debt overnight either. Both situations take time and effort to change. The larger the debt problem, the longer it will take to work through it. But instead of focusing on how long it will take you to repay your debts, focus instead on how wonderful it will feel when you are completely free. Celebrate small victories along the way so you will not get discouraged as you work toward your ultimate goal.

Consumer debt is a form of slavery you can avoid. Get rid of indebtedness for good so you can experience the freedom and clarity of not being at the mercy of lenders.

CLUTTER *BUSTERS*

◆ If your family is in debt, what are some of the ways in which your lives and your relationships are affected by the debt?

◆ How would your life look if you were debt free? What would you do that you can't do now? Likewise, what wouldn't you do that you must do now?

◆ Could God be saying to you what he told Leimome: "Pack your bags; get ready to go"? If God called you to a new area of ministry or service today, would your debt hinder you from responding to that call?

COMING INTO CLARITY

I was one of many individuals caught in the credit card trap and trying to keep up with what other family members had. What's funny about that is, the more I spent, the emptier I was. So I started reading everything about being frugal, gave up unnecessary spending, developed a budget, and completely changed my way of thinking about my needs.

It was hard giving up the fancy dry cleaners and buying clothes on a whim. Now I purchase only what I need. My family tells me to buy a new car every time they see me, but my car runs and it's paid for! A coworker bragged about how he drives a Lexus, and I wondered how he could afford it. Then one day he told me he had borrowed all he could from his retirement account to buy it. I felt so sad for him. People don't realize that God can't reach us if we are buried under worldly desires and possessions. I learned that if you are stressed by your lifestyle, it may be because God is trying to reach you and you're not paying attention!

Linda
Parkville, Maryland

SIXTEEN

GOOD-BYE, CLUTTER!
*Away with sluggish giving! I'm tired of holding back.
I'd like to give as freely as God has given to me.*

the
paradox
of giving

*O*ne of my family's favorite holiday movies is *The Polar Express*, the 2004 computer-animated film featuring the vocal talents of Tom Hanks. The story is about a young boy who has almost given up on the idea of Santa Claus. Then on Christmas Eve, he is invited to take an incredible magical train ride to the North Pole to meet Santa in person.

During his adventure, the boy—whose name we never learn—makes new friends, one of whom is a child named Billy. Billy had his doubts about Santa too, but for different reasons. Billy's family is poor, so he has never experienced Christmas as other children have.

For me, one of the most memorable parts of the movie is seeing how Billy reacts when he discovers his name and address on a big, brightly wrapped package in Santa's workshop. Billy has never received a Christmas gift before, so from that moment forward he is determined to keep that package with him, no matter what.

Near the end of the movie, an elf asks Billy to give him the package so it can be loaded onto Santa's sleigh with all the other presents. Billy hesitates and ponders his choices. If he doesn't let go of the package, Santa can't deliver it to his house on Christmas morning. If he does let go, how can he trust he will really see it again? Reluctantly, Billy releases his grasp on the gift and hopes he won't be disappointed. When the Polar Express drops him off at his house at the end of the trip, Billy finds that Santa has already stopped by. The gift is waiting for him.

Giving is a paradox. Instead of experiencing loss when we give, we experience gain.

Don't we all sometimes hold on so tightly to the gifts God has given us? When it comes to giving, we seem to be afraid to let go. Like Billy, we're hesitant to entrust the gifts back into the hands of the one who gave them to us in the first place. Do you want to give to your church or favorite ministry but never manage to actually do it on a regular basis? Does giving 10 percent or more of your income seem like an impossibility—something only the wealthy can afford to do? Are you afraid that if you do give that much, you won't have enough left over to pay your bills?

Giving is a paradox. Instead of experiencing loss when we give, we experience gain. Sometimes what we receive back is money—maybe an unexpected bonus at work or a tax refund that was a surprise, a promotion at work, or an investment that does better than we'd hoped. The blessing we gain could be that our limited resources go much further than they would otherwise. At other times what we receive is not material but emotional or spiritual: the satisfaction of helping others; the feeling of prosperity that comes from sharing; and the knowledge that even if we don't see immediate rewards here on earth, we will be rewarded in Heaven.

Sometimes we don't give because we think we can't afford to. Ironically, the secret of giving is that we can't afford *not* to.

MINE!

Often when Lydia and I are out running errands, she gets hungry and asks me to buy her some sort of treat. Occasionally I ask her to share some of her snack with me. Lydia has been known to develop a sudden case of amnesia when this happens. She can't seem to recall who paid for the snack or why it was given to her in the first place. Instead of recognizing my generosity and being happy to share, all she can say is, "It's mine!" She's afraid that if she shares there won't be enough left for her.

That's the same lie Satan wants us to believe when we think about giving. He loves to play on our fears and insecurities with thoughts of whether we can afford to give. Our enemy wants us to look at all our financial worries and wonder how we can possibly give. He wants us to focus on our own limited resources rather than trusting in God's infinite resources. This deception is a powerful one, because when we fall for it and don't give, we actually accomplish another of Satan's purposes: we stand in the way of God's blessings being shared with others through us.

God's desire is to bless us and to bless others through us, but he cannot fully bless us unless we trust him enough to let go.

GOD'S MEASURING CUP

If you've been a Christian for any length of time, you have undoubtedly heard the word *tithing* used interchangeably with *giving*. But *tithe* simply means a tenth. In the Old Testament, God required his people to give an offering of 10 percent of all their crops and flocks. Jewish law was very specific about how much to give, when to give, and what was to be done with the offering once it was given.

In the New Testament, no such specifics are given. Jesus never issued direct commands about exactly how much to give, but he did say to give without reservation: "Give, and it will be given to you. A good measure, pressed down, shaken together and running over, will be poured into your lap. For with the measure you use, it will be measured to you" (Luke 6:38). The apostle Paul wrote: "Each man should give what he has decided in his heart to give, not reluctantly or under compulsion, for God loves a cheerful giver" (2 Corinthians 9:7).

God doesn't need your money; what he wants is your heart. He wants you to trust him and give your "good measure" cheerfully, knowing whatever you entrust to him will be given back many times over in the form of blessings.

The truth is that God is not as concerned about the particulars as we seem to be. He is more interested in giving that is both faithful and faith filled. This kind of giving is what the third part of the Clarity Principle is all about: "Let us fix our eyes on Jesus." When it comes to giving, we don't have to wonder what Jesus would do. We can look at what he did: Jesus gave his life. What more could he possibly offer? If he gave everything he had for us, shouldn't we give everything we can back to him?

As he did in the Old Testament, God could have demanded that Christians give a certain percentage, but he chose not to. He wants us to give out of gratitude, not requirement. And when we do, it brings him great joy to open the floodgates with even more of the good things he has to offer.

WHY DON'T WE GIVE?

If you ask a group of Christian women whether they think it is important to give, probably nearly all of them will say yes. But then ask each woman whether she gives as much and as often as she would like to, and watch the number of affirmative answers go down. If we believe giving is important, why don't more of us give as generously or as regularly as we would like?

Jesus never issued direct commands about exactly how much to give, but he did say to give without reservation.

Some of us don't give because of fear—fear of letting go or fear of putting our finances into God's hands. As women, we have a natural inclination to put our own families' needs first. If your family is already struggling financially, it may be difficult to see how giving away some of what little you have could actually make the situation better.

Another reason that our giving may lag behind our good intentions is that we do not plan to give. We aren't disciplined about it. When you don't have some sort of written budget to guide how your income is spent, you have no way of knowing where your money is going. You may truly want to give on a regular basis, but unless giving is part of your financial plan, God ends up with the leftovers.

Yet giving is a can't-lose proposition. Regular giving clarifies life because it opens the door for God to move on our behalf in ways we would never experience otherwise. In Malachi 3:10 God states, "Bring the whole tithe into the storehouse. . . . Test me in this . . . and see if I will not throw open the floodgates of heaven and pour out so much blessing that you will not have room enough for it." Life is hard enough; why would we want to complicate it by going without God's protection, provision, and blessings? Why hold back when we know God won't hold back on us when we are willing to give?

You Can Become a Cheerful Giver!

I have a good friend who is truly a cheerful giver. Angel lives with her husband, Ron, and two cats in one room of a house they share with her father-in-law. Angel and Ron had problems with debt in the past, but now they are debt free and committed to staying that way, no matter what.

Angel and her husband both have physical challenges and are unable to work. The cost of their medications is high, and what's left over from their combined disability income isn't much. If ever a family had an excuse not to give, it would certainly be Angel and Ron, yet they are two of the most giving people I know.

In addition to giving 10 percent of their monthly income to their church, they feel a special burden for single moms. Each time a situation arises for which they feel called to give, they pray about it and then proceed with giving, even when it appears they don't have enough money to do so. Over and over the Lord has provided when they stepped out in faith.

How does someone go from giving sporadically or sluggishly to giving as consistently and conscientiously as Angel and Ron do? These strategies will help:

Objectively examine your current giving habits. Ask yourself: Am I giving a "good measure" or just whatever happens to be left over? Do I have a written budget to help me make sure my giving is based on reality, not merely on good intentions?

Is fear holding me back from giving as much as I'd like? If it's not fear, what is it? Be honest with yourself and with God. Ask God to show you the difference between where you are now and where he would like you to be in your giving.

USE A BUDGET TO BE PURPOSEFUL IN GIVING. If financial worries—debt, overspending, lack of income—are holding you back from giving, a written budget is critical to help regulate where your money is going. A budget will keep you on track to give conscientiously, if that budget includes a certain portion per pay period allotted specifically for giving. It will also help you be consistent, because seeing funds accumulate in the giving category of your budget will remind you to make your contributions. If your current budget does not include a category for giving (or if the allotment is smaller than you'd like), review your budget to see where you can cut back to free up additional funds for giving. If you need help with budgeting, see the Resources section at the end of this book.

Ask God to show you the difference between where you are now and where he would like you to be in your giving.

STRATEGICALLY PLAN YOUR INCREASE. Once you've decided to increase your giving, decide by how much. One way to begin is to start small and work your way up. If you are currently giving an average of 5 percent of your income but want to eventually give 10 percent, bump up your giving by one percent every few months until you reach that goal. This will help you acclimate to each increase before making another one.

The little-at-a-time approach works, but things get really exciting when you decide to step out in faith and put God's promises to the test. So another possibility is to just decide what increase you want to make and go for it! If you decide to take this approach, prepare to be amazed at all the ways God will provide and reward you for your step of faith.

LOOK FOR CREATIVE WAYS TO GIVE. But what about the person who is deeply in debt? As a Christian, you are called to give, but you are also legally and biblically obligated to fulfill your financial obligations. You can still make giving a priority, even if you cannot give as much as you'd like right now. If you are willing to sacrifice, you can almost always find ways to free up funds that could be used for giving. What could you give up or cut back on in order to have something to give? Could you serve vegetarian meals one or two days a week and give the money you would have spent on meat? Could you carpool to work with a neighbor and give the money you save on gas? Even small amounts are pleasing to God when given with a cheerful heart and obedient spirit. If there is simply no way to give of your money, look for ways to give of your time.

PRAYERFULLY FOLLOW GOD'S LEADING. Ask God how much you should give and where he wants the money to go. Your home congregation is a good place to start, but maybe he would have you support other ministries as well. Since it all belongs to him anyway, ask him to make clear to you how he wants the money to be used.

Has skimpy giving caused you to miss out on the bountiful blessings God has in store for you? Are you ready to receive God's good measure, running over and pouring into your lap? If so, say good-bye to your old giving habits and say hello to the security and clarity of God's plan for giving.

CLUTTER *BUSTERS*

◆ What blessings have you received as a result of giving?

◆ Luke 6:38 says, "For with the measure you use, it will be measured to you." How have your decisions to give or not give impacted the extent to which God has blessed you?

◆ When you think about Jesus' love for you and his death on the cross, how do you feel about your own giving? Are you inspired and challenged to give more than you currently do? How will you make that goal a reality?

COMING INTO CLARITY

My husband and I have been married thirty-nine years, and we have always given at least 10 percent of our gross income to the Lord. At times we have lived paycheck to paycheck, but we have never done without anything we needed.

We built our house in 1979 and had two young daughters. We continued to tithe even though we had taken on what at the time seemed like an enormous house payment. We paid off our thirty-year mortgage in twenty years, and have always reaped the benefits of regular giving. In 1994, my husband became disabled and has not worked since. Through these years God has blessed us with tremendous blessings.

I retired in 2003, and we continue to give at least 10 percent. As far as we are concerned, our giving is treated just as any other monthly bill that we owe. That check is written the first of each month since that is when we get paid. I cannot emphasize enough the blessing of giving to God, both with money and time.

Mary Ann
Oliver Springs, Tennessee

SEVENTEEN

GOOD-BYE, CLUTTER!
No more looking to money to solve my problems. I don't want to give money that place of prominence in my life anymore.

---

what
money
cannot do

When Michael and I lived in Memphis, we had the privilege of attending a small church of only twenty families. One of the things that made this church special was that the members didn't pay lip service to the idea of bearing one another's burdens. They actually did it! Each Sunday a portion of the worship service was designated as sharing time. Anyone from the youngest to the oldest could share whatever was on his heart.

Jo attended this church with her children. During the time we knew Jo, she had gone through many difficulties: health issues, teenagers in trouble, a crumbling marriage, and then a financial crisis when her husband finally left for good. But most devastating of all was when Jo faced every parent's worst nightmare: one of her teens tried to commit suicide.

Jo shared the details of how her son tried to end his life by overdosing on weight-loss pills. We all cried with her as she described the guilt and sense of helplessness she felt. Thank God her son survived, but Jo was left with the task of putting her and her children's lives back together.

Several months after her son's suicide attempt, Jo told the group that all the hardship her family went through had changed her perspective about life's problems. "Now I know what my daddy used to say is true," Jo explained. "He always said, 'If you've got problems money will solve, you don't have problems.'"

Jo had faced all sorts of challenges in her life, but most of them had nothing to do with money. Money couldn't restore her marriage or keep her kids out of trouble. It couldn't heal her illnesses or make her son emotionally healthy. Money could pay her bills, but compared to all the other issues in her life, paying rent was the least of Jo's worries.

Jo's father was a wise man. He understood that money does not have the power to meet our deepest needs or heal our deepest hurts; it's not a cure-all. The modern mind-set is that if we throw enough money at any problem, the problem will go away. Sadly, the opposite is usually true: throwing money at a problem often brings more heartache in the long run.

---

*"If you've got problems money will solve,
you don't have problems."*

Do you often try to spend your way out of problems? Are you frequently faced with unexpected new challenges because you tried to take the easy way out instead of making the necessary changes to solve the original problem? We live in an instant-download society; we want everything quick and easy. We don't want to wait, and we certainly don't want to have to change our own behavior. Money becomes our hero because we think it can buy us the immediate results we're looking for.

MONEY IS a TOOL

Michael and I have had the privilege of attending a money-management seminar by author and financial expert Dave Ramsey. During his presentation, Dave picked up a brick that was sitting at the side of the stage. Holding it high so everyone could see, he asked, "Is this brick good or evil?"

While the audience pondered his question, Dave explained himself. Bricks are inanimate objects. They are neither good nor evil. You can use a brick for something beneficial, like building a house, or for something hurtful, like smashing a window. A brick is simply a tool. In the same way, money is neither good nor evil. As a tool, it only has the power to do what you use it to do.

If money is only a tool, where did we get the idea that money has power to solve all our problems? This deception is rooted in one of our enemy's favorite strategies. Throughout this book, we've seen that Satan's goal is to keep us looking to anything and anyone but God for help. Money can buy temporary pleasures and quick fixes, but it cannot bring lasting relief from the real issues that trouble us. As long as we look to money to solve our problems, we promote it to the status of deliverer—a distinction God alone deserves. Satan knows that by chasing after quick and easy answers, we forfeit the help that can be ours if we depend on God for his answers on his timetable.

Do you remember the Old Testament account of the Israelites creating and worshiping a golden calf? Exodus 32 tells us that the Israelites grew impatient while waiting for Moses to return from meeting with God on Mount Sinai. They decided to take matters into their own hands. Instead of waiting for God's leadership, they made an idol and called it their god.

How could they possibly imagine that a lifeless piece of metal could take care of them better than God could? The whole thing sounds ludicrous until we realize we are often guilty of exactly the same thing. An idol doesn't have to be a statue of gold. An idol is anything that takes the place of God in our lives—anything we think can give us what only God can truly provide.

"We don't build golden calves anymore," dietician Gwen Shamblin used to say in her weight-loss books and tapes, "but we do carve out a pan of brownies and say, 'Oh pan of brownies, you calm my nerves.' Or, 'Oh pan of brownies, you ease my pain. Oh brownies, you help me forget my troubles.'"[1] Just as food can become a god to us, so can money. When we use it to bypass our dependence on God, we worship it as an idol and take ourselves even further from God's help and provision.

YOU CAN'T SERVE GOD and MONEY

With all the modern conveniences and technology at our disposal, the temptation is great to put our hope in money's ability to make everything right. But even people in Jesus' day needed to hear about the dangers of this kind of thinking.

An idol is anything that takes the place of God in our lives—anything we think can give us what only God can truly provide.

Jesus said, "No one can serve two masters. Either he will hate the one and love the other, or he will be devoted to the one and despise the other. You cannot serve both God and Money"

(Matthew 6:24). Jesus didn't say you shouldn't. He said you *can't*. In other words, you have to choose between the two. If you rely on one in your time of need, you forfeit the possibility of relying on the other. It's an either-or proposition.

Let's put this in concrete terms. What are some of the ways we make a god of money? Have you tried to conquer feelings of inadequacy by pursuing every possible degree or certification in your field? Do you ever try to deal with your kids' behavior problems by enrolling them in another class or sports activity? Are you so desperate to lose weight that you're a sucker for every new diet product on the market? Instead of asking for and waiting for God's guidance to address the real issues, we rely on the quick-fix solutions we think money can buy.

My friend Amy shared a few of the ways she has noticed herself and her friends looking to money to solve their problems. Amy truly wants a clearer, simpler, more peaceful lifestyle for her family, but on more than one occasion she has spent $250 on wicker baskets because she thought that having more baskets to hold things would somehow magically make her house more organized. She soon realized that all the baskets in the world would not solve the real issue.

"What I really need to do is change my daily habits," Amy told me. "I need to clean up immediately after each meal, put my supplies away immediately when a project is finished, and help the children pick up their toys right away when an activity ends."

Amy also has observed several friends spend large amounts of money on exercise machines because they were desperate to lose weight. "They signed on the dotted line, hauled the mammoth devices home, and felt so proud of themselves that evening," Amy said. "But one or two years later, the machines are dusty, and my friends still weigh the same."

As Amy points out, purchases rarely solve problems. Think back to the second part of the Clarity Principle: "Let us run with perseverance the race marked out for us." God is the giver of all good things—including your money. But the gift can never replace the giver. Using money to solve difficulties only complicates life because it's the wrong tool for the job. Just as a bandage won't fix a broken leg, things that money can buy won't fix the gaping wounds of life. Looking to God as your healer simplifies life because he is the only one who can truly provide the far-reaching answers and permanent solutions you need.

PUTTING MONEY in ITS PLACE

Nothing boosts self-confidence like knowing you look your best—or at least that's what I thought. A couple of years ago, I was going into the busy season in my ministry. I had begun teaching on a new topic that year and was feeling a little unsure of myself.

Maybe if I had something sharp to wear I'd feel better, I thought as I purchased a beautiful baby-blue business suit.

The suit was on sale, so I convinced myself that it was just what I needed to help me look and sound like someone speaking with confidence. I was quite proud of my purchase until I got it home and began to think through exactly what I would wear with my new power suit.

First, there was the issue of shoes—I didn't own any that would match. Then I looked at my jewelry selection. This suit definitely needed power accessories! And then there was the little problem of the suit's V-neck. I would need some sort of camisole underneath.

Although the suit was reasonably priced, I realized this ensemble of self-confidence was going to end up costing me royally. I worried for days about how to complete my look without spending a small fortune, before I realized I was trying to spend my way out of my lack of self-assurance. Poise comes from within. If I didn't feel it on the inside, all the fancy clothes in the world wouldn't make me look like I had it on the outside. Instead of trying to put together the perfect outfit, I needed to entrust the matter to God, relying on him to provide the inner peace and security I needed. When I thought about it that way, I realized the suit wasn't such a good deal after all, and I returned it for a refund.

Have you depended more on money than God to solve your problems? If so, here's what you can do about it:

DIG BENEATH THE SURFACE. Recognize that when you feel tempted to throw money at a problem, there almost always are deeper issues that need to be addressed. Maybe negative feelings or unhealthy obsessions are driving your behavior. Or maybe laziness or fear of failure is causing you to try to avoid the difficult task of changing old habits. Ask God to show you what the underlying issues are.

SEEK GOD'S HELP. After you've identified what's really going on, ask God to help you. If habits need to change, ask the Lord to empower you to make those changes. Is the issue insecurity, impatience, or unwillingness to relinquish the problem to God's care? Ask God to help you deal with those challenges so they no longer control the way you react to problems. In addition to God's help, you may also need to seek counsel from other sources of support: nutritional planning from a registered dietician, guidance on parenting from a Christian parenting class, or career counseling from a career coach, for example.

SAFEGUARD YOURSELF AGAINST SETBACKS. Once you've submitted this aspect of your life to God and have begun working to change, be on the lookout for areas in which old attitudes may subtly sneak in again. The point is not that you should never spend money as part of the solution to a problem. The issue is trying to take matters into your own hands instead of putting them into God's hands. Be watchful for times when the temptation seems particularly strong to go after a quick fix on your own.

Are you tired of compounding problems by trying to take the easy way out? Are you ready to break an unhealthy dependency on money so you can be fully dependent on God? If so, now is the time to walk away from these habits once and for all. Strip money of its golden-calf status and clarify life by relying on the only true God.

◐ CLUTTER *BUSTERS* ◑

◆ Why do you think we look to money as an answer to many of life's problems?

◆ When have you tried to spend your way out of a problem but found that you only made the problem worse?

◆ Instead of waiting for God's help and leadership, the Israelites made a golden calf and looked to it to deliver them. What "golden calves" are common in our culture? Are any of them present in your life?

COMING INTO CLARITY

My years of being a young homemaker were a time when aspirations were high, self-esteem was vulnerable, and money was carefully stretched. During that time I began browsing through women's magazines regularly for home decorating ideas because I wanted to achieve the look and style I envied in other women's homes. These magazines showed all the latest ways to make my home look good—and how to spend more money to do it. I eventually realized that looking to the magazines for inspiration was really just fueling a spirit of discontentment in me. I prayed about it and decided I needed to avoid those magazines altogether.

After that prayerful decision, the Lord gave me many (and far better!) creative resources through personal relationships, especially with several wonderful women in my church. The Lord wanted me to use and develop my abilities for his glory. He used these women to teach and inspire me with creative, efficient, and economical ideas. A battle with discontent was turned into a process of keeping my focus on the Lord and what he wanted me to do with what he had given me.

Martha
Seattle, Washington

Above all else, guard your heart, for it is the wellspring of life.
PROVERBS 4:23

---

guard
your heart

I first heard Proverbs 4:23 more than a decade ago, when Michael and I were newlyweds and I was working outside the home. At the time, I was having problems at work. Several new employees recently had been hired in my department. Rumor had it that these new employees were given much higher salaries than the rest of us.

I didn't want to feel resentful about this, but the truth was, I did. The inequity seemed unjust. The owners of the company were Christians whom I respected as brothers and sisters in Christ. I wanted to trust that they had good reasons for their decisions, yet I couldn't help but feel mistreated. I didn't want this situation to affect my job performance, so I talked to Terry, the company's employee counselor, about it.

His advice? "Go talk to your boss. Don't let this issue fester inside you." Then he directed me to Proverbs 4:23: "Above all else, guard your heart, for it is the wellspring of life." Terry reminded me that keeping my heart clean and pure was my first priority. If I allowed unhealthy emotions like anger, resentment, and disrespect to lurk in my heart, all other areas of life—including my job performance—would suffer.

So I took Terry's advice and made an appointment to speak with my manager. After hearing her side of the story and voicing my own, I felt much more peaceful about the situation. Our working relationship was strengthened as a result of this open and honest exchange.

The premise of this book from page one has been that we can't serve God wholeheartedly and with clarity when our hearts are cluttered. If we allow clutter to fill our hearts, all areas of life will be affected. My goal for this book is to equip you to guard your heart.

The way Proverbs 4:23 reads in other translations also appeals to me: "Keep vigilant watch over your heart; *that's* where life starts" (*The Message*). "Keep your heart pure for out of it are the important things of life" (*NLV*). "Above all else, guard your heart, for it affects everything you do" (*NLT*).

How do you handle your time and possessions? How you do deal with your money? What thoughts control your mind? All of these are determined by what's in your heart. That's why heart matters matter. And that's why any attempt to declutter your life must first start on the inside with a thorough cleaning of your heart.

Dietrich Bonhoeffer was a German theologian who was executed by the Nazis for taking a stand against Hitler's regime. Bonhoeffer wrote, "To be simple is to fix one's eyes solely on the simple truth of God at a time when all concepts are being confused, distorted, and turned upside down."[1]

Confused.

Distorted.

Upside down.

Do these words describe life in your corner of the world? I've been there too. But the good news is that we don't have to wallow in the confusion and distortion. We can remain right side up even when the world around us flips over, under, and back. We can tune out the static of day-to-day life and tune in to the simple truths God gives us in his Word.

Years ago I was busily preparing to travel to another state where I was scheduled to speak to a group of Christian teachers about the joys and blessings of living simply. Ironically, things were far from simple in my home that day. The phone rang repeatedly. My e-mail inbox filled with messages. Michael interrupted me several times to ask for help. No matter how hard I tried to concentrate, my train of thought was repeatedly derailed. I wanted to scream.

Frustrated and on the verge of tears, I looked at Michael and said, "I'm a fine one to be teaching about simplicity! Life sure doesn't feel very simple right now."

I wanted to keep my life simple, but I couldn't do it by my own power. It wasn't until I stepped back, took a deep breath, and asked for God's help that I regained my focus and composure.

As I realized on that hectic day several years ago, simplicity is a gift God graciously gives, because only he can enable us to fully experience it. More than our own willpower is required in order to live simply. Without God's guidance I can't stay grounded when the world around me is a whirlwind. I can't place the important before the trivial without God's power to help me do so. Without God's intervention, I am a helpless victim of all the chaos Satan uses to keep my eyes off God and on the mess around me.

Since that time, my prayer has been, "Lord, help me to live simply." That's my prayer for myself—to live a simple, uncluttered life of clarity—and that's my prayer for you.

working relationship was strengthened as a result of this open and honest exchange.

The premise of this book from page one has been that we can't serve God wholeheartedly and with clarity when our hearts are cluttered. If we allow clutter to fill our hearts, all areas of life will be affected. My goal for this book is to equip you to guard your heart.

The way Proverbs 4:23 reads in other translations also appeals to me: "Keep vigilant watch over your heart; *that's* where life starts" (*The Message*). "Keep your heart pure for out of it are the important things of life" (*NLV*). "Above all else, guard your heart, for it affects everything you do" (*NLT*).

How do you handle your time and possessions? How you do deal with your money? What thoughts control your mind? All of these are determined by what's in your heart. That's why heart matters matter. And that's why any attempt to declutter your life must first start on the inside with a thorough cleaning of your heart.

Dietrich Bonhoeffer was a German theologian who was executed by the Nazis for taking a stand against Hitler's regime. Bonhoeffer wrote, "To be simple is to fix one's eyes solely on the simple truth of God at a time when all concepts are being confused, distorted, and turned upside down."[1]

Confused.

Distorted.

Upside down.

Do these words describe life in your corner of the world? I've been there too. But the good news is that we don't have to wallow in the confusion and distortion. We can remain right

✦ RESOURCES ✦

Crown Financial Ministries

Founded by financial experts Howard Dayton and the late Larry Burkett, this ministry offers programs that teach biblical principles of finances. Resources include radio programs, small-group programs, newsletters, books, workbooks, and software.

Web: http://www.crown.org
Crown Financial Ministries, P.O. Box 100, Gainesville, GA 30503-0100
Phone: (800) 722-1976

Financial Peace University

Founded by financial expert Dave Ramsey, Financial Peace University is a thirteen-week program that teaches participants how to reduce debt and achieve financial goals. Resources also include *The Dave Ramsey Show* radio program, books, software, and products to help teach children about money management.

Web: http://www.daveramsey.com
The Lampo Group, 1749 Mallory Lane, Suite 100, Brentwood, TN 37027
Phone: (888) 227-3223

Good $ense Ministry

Founded by the Willow Creek Community Church, Good $ense is a financial stewardship ministry that helps churches teach and train their members how to honor God with their resources. Includes a budgeting course and budget counseling training.

Web: http://www.goodsenseministry.com
Willow Creek Association, P.O. Box 3188, Barrington, IL 60011-3188
Phone: (847) 765-0070

Generous Giving

A nonprofit educational organization, the mission of Generous Giving is to motivate followers of Jesus Christ toward greater biblical generosity. Resources include books, study guides, curricula, newsletters, and an online research library.

Web: http://www.generousgiving.org
Generous Giving, 820 Broad St., Suite 300, Chattanooga, TN 37402
Phone: (423) 755-2399

✦ NOTES ✦

Stewardship Is More Than Giving

1. Benjamin Franklin, QuoteDB, http://www.quotedb.com/quotes/987 (accessed April 27, 2007).

Sweet Freedom

1. "Lagging Behind the Wealthy, Many Use Debt to Catch Up," *The Wall Street Journal Online*, May 17, 2005, http://www.econ.upenn.edu/~dkrueger/press/WSJ.pdf (accessed April 27, 2007).

What Money Cannot Do

1. Gwen Shamblin, "Emotional Eating," *Rising Above the Magnetic Pull of the Refrigerator*, audio cassette (Franklin, TN: The Weigh Down Workshop, Inc., 1992).

Guard Your Heart

1. Dietrich Bonhoeffer, *Ethics*, ed. Eberhard Bethge, trans. Neville Horton Smith, 4th printing (New York: The Macmillan Company, 1961), 7.